TAKE PART
Speaking Canadian English
Second Edition

Lucia Pietrusiak Engkent   Karen P. Bardy

Prentice-Hall Canada Inc., Scarborough, Ontario

Canadian Cataloguing in Publication Data

Engkent, Lucia Pietrusiak, 1955—
   Take part: speaking Canadian English

2nd ed.
ISBN 0-13-882275-1

1. English language—Canada—Text-books for
second language learners.* 2. English language—
Spoken English—Canada. 3. Canadianisms (English).*
I. Bardy, Karen P., 1954- . II. Title.

PE1128.E54 1992   428.3'4   C91-095535-2

Prentice-Hall, Inc., Englewood Cliffs, New Jersey
Prentice-Hall International, Inc., London
Prentice-Hall of Australia, Pty., Ltd., Sydney
Prentice-Hall of India Pvt., Ltd., New Delhi
Prentice-Hall of Japan, Inc., Tokyo
Prentice-Hall of Southeast Asia (Pte.) Ltd., Singapore
Editora Prentice-Hall do Brasil Ltda., Rio de Janeiro
Prentice-Hall Hispanoamericana, S.A., Mexico

ISBN 0-13-882275-1

Acquisitions editor: Marjorie Walker
Developmental editor: Linda Gorman
Production editor: Elynor Kagan
Production coordinator: Anna Orodi
Design and composition: Anita Macklin
Illustrations: Tami Hadley and Marjorie Pearson
Cover design: Aurora Di Ciaula
Cover illustration: Marjorie Pearson

2 3 4 5 MP 96 95 94 93
Printed and bound in Canada by Maracle Press

TABLE OF CONTENTS

PREFACE

Take Part: Speaking Canadian English focuses on the language and culture of everyday Canadian life. It has been designed to meet the needs of adult intermediate students, especially those who have a good grasp of formal English but have difficulty with informal language. The book offers insights into the way the language is spoken everyday and gives students the opportunity to practise speaking on a variety of topics. In addition, cultural information prepares students for social life in Canada.

Take Part can be used either on its own for conversation courses or as a supplementary text for multi-skill and intensive courses. It was developed as a 40-hour intermediate conversation course for adults, many of whom were foreign students or new immigrants who had studied English before coming to Canada.

Conversational English

Register, the language appropriate to a particular context, is a very important part of language use. *Take Part* focuses on the conversational register of everyday English and explains what characterizes it and how it is different from more formal English. Because of this focus, there are no writing assignments in the text. However, if the book is used in a multi-skills course, the discussion topics can be given as essay assignments.

Informal conversational English is often very difficult for students to understand and use correctly. What language learners hear native speakers saying often does not conform to the formal descriptions of English found in textbooks. Moreover, informal spoken English changes more quickly than written English. Slang expressions, for example, come in and out of fashion. Even if students do not use certain colloquialisms in their speech, they need a thorough understanding of the forms and principles involved.

One of the problems in dealing with conversational English is the question of a standard. Where do we draw the line between standard colloquial English and non-standard English, or between idiom and slang? What do we consider a vulgarism and what is grammatical "pickiness"?

As teachers and writers, we have had to draw the line ourselves. Others may disagree with us. For example, we have used the frequently heard, but technically ungrammatical, "here's" and "there's" with plural subjects — aiming for a standard conversational style of English. Forms that would be inappropriate in formal situations are marked as colloquial or slang.

By treating formal and informal English as distinct varieties, teachers can explain to the students that what they hear native speakers say in conversation is correct in that situation, but does not belong in an essay, for example. In this way, students do not see the language in absolutes — black or white, right or wrong. Colloquial English is a living, changing thing; forms that are considered non-standard today may gradually become accepted. Both teachers and students must accept forms in common usage and yet be aware of factors of social acceptability in language.

Much of conversational English is too subtle to describe in written form. Teachers must use their own judgement in explaining shades of meaning in tone of voice and gestures. Context and situation can change the meaning of an utterance. Regional variations in vocabulary or social contexts must also be taken into account.

Organization

Take Part: Speaking Canadian English is divided into sixteen units that deal with topics of everyday conversation. The units focus on such themes as health and fitness, adult education, leisure activities, government and travel and tourism. Various linguistic and cultural aspects of each theme are explored. Depending on the interest and needs of the students, each unit may take two to several hours to complete.

The units do not have to be studied sequentially, since the text does not depend on a gradation of structures and vocabulary. There is, however, a sense of progression in the text. The organization is thematic. Early units treat topics such as introductions and casual small talk, while later units explore more complex subjects, such as the Canadian political structure. The text ends with a unit on telephone calls, a particular type of conversation.

This type of organization allows each unit to stand on its own; the teacher can choose and order the lessons according to the needs and interests of a particular class. The thematic organization means that each unit can lead to a further exploration of the topic in a wider context and that it can be integrated into existing ESL curricula.

Each unit follows essentially the same pattern: dialogues and texts introduce the topic, language notes follow up on structures and expressions used in the dialogues, a culture note explains other aspects of the theme. New to the second edition is a structured activity that follows the culture note in each unit. Additional vocabulary then prepares the students to deal with the discussion topics, activities and assignments at the end of the unit.

Since there is a great deal of material and many activities, teachers are encouraged to make selections appropriate to the needs and interests of the particular class and to vary the types of activities used. For one unit, the class may do a number of role plays; for another, they may have a discussion or debate on the topic.

Considering the wide variety of ESL teaching situations in Canada, we have tried to leave teachers and students many options. Not only will the needs and interests of the students influence many of the teacher's choices, but also the time and facilities available will determine what is actually done in the classroom and how it is done. Therefore, many of the activities are left open-ended, ready for the teacher's specifications. Some of the material can also be used for self-study by the students.

Dialogues

The theme of each chapter is introduced by dialogues that illustrate typical conversations on the subject at hand and provide a context for many idiomatic expressions and different vocabulary items. Each dialogue provides models for informal conversation and stimulates further discussion. The dialogues are simply a point of departure for the classwork and do not have to be memorized by the students.

Each dialogue is introduced with a paragraph that sets the scene or explains some of the cultural assumptions in the situation. These explanatory paragraphs are new to the second edition.

Vocabulary notes are found in the margins next to the dialogues. These explain, for the most part, idiomatic words and expressions or unusual uses of words. Vocabulary items that may prove difficult for the students, but have straightforward dictionary definitions, are generally not explained in the notes.

There is no continuing cast of characters in the dialogues; rather, characters are named with a variety of first names. In the first edition, English names were used in order to give students the opportunity to learn as many common names as possible. In the second edition, many of the names have been changed and are now drawn from a variety of ethnic backgrounds. This mix of names reflects the reality of life in Canada, where students will have to learn to use names from many languages.

The names should not be treated as belonging exclusively to one nationality or another; a famous example of a name that does not belong to the bearer's own ethnic background is Pierre Trudeau's son Sasha, whose name is the Russian short form for Alexander. In addition, many immigrants choose English names for themselves or their children. Therefore, teachers and students should not assume that the use of a certain name means that the character is necessarily of a certain ethnic group.

A discussion section follows each dialogue and includes comprehension questions, discussion topics and class activities. The comprehension questions do not follow all the action or statements in the dialogues; rather, they focus on extra-linguistic factors. Teachers may wish to ask their students more direct questions to ensure that they are following the dialogue.

In addition to the dialogues, other passages are used to introduce the topic and are accompanied by vocabulary notes and discussion questions. These include prose passages, such as the descriptions of Canadian holidays and the letter to an advice column, or monologues, such as the television commercials and news announcements.

Language Notes

The language notes are based on examples in the dialogues and focus on features of informal English. Thus, instead of following a structural syllabus, we have let the material itself dictate which structures and forms will be explored. The language notes follow up on forms and expressions used in the dialogues and explain or expand on them. There are four main kinds of language notes: notes on grammatical structures, notes on pronunciation, notes on idioms and notes on functions.

It is assumed that the students at this level will have an understanding of basic English grammar. The grammar-based language notes, therefore, are brief descriptions. Some of the notes review structures that the students have studied, but may look at them in a different light — in the context of conversational usage. The notes highlight the differences between formal and informal English, especially where these differences may mean that rules of formal grammar are "broken." For example, the language note on tag questions focuses on their conversational function and their intonation patterns.

The pronunciation notes focus mainly on stress and intonation. Notes on idioms clarify confusing sets of idioms, showing a pattern where possible. Functional language notes show how certain forms are used for specific functions.

In the second edition, some of the more general language notes on pronunciation have been eliminated. These include notes on the pronunciation of -s and -ed endings and basic stress patterns in sentences. It is assumed that the teacher will cover these features when necessary in any course that deals with spoken English.

Most of the new language notes in the second edition focus on groups of idioms. Instead of always following an example found in a dialogue, some of these are linked to the theme of the unit. For example, Unit 15, "The Marketplace," includes a language note on idioms using money terms.

Culture Notes

The culture notes either focus on a particular aspect of the topic of the chapter or help to add ideas to the general discussion. They do not explain "rules of behaviour," but offer some insights into the attitudes, customs and lifestyles of Canadians.

There are no notes and questions directly accompanying the culture notes. A general class discussion should clear up any comprehension difficulties. In addition, the last sections of the unit — Additional Vocabulary, Discussion Topics, Additional Activities and Assignments — follow up on many of the issues raised in the culture notes.

The culture notes have been revised and updated for the second edition. More controversial issues have been introduced for the students to discuss. Descriptions of culture are always subjective, so different interpretations may be brought out in class discussion. Rather than viewing these negatively as contradictions, students and teachers can benefit from conflicting views by engaging in lively discussion.

Activities

The major additions to the second edition are structured activities for each unit. These are usually games, simulations or problem-solving activities. These activities can be used with students with different levels of language proficiency; lower level students will simply not be able to perform them with the degree of sophistication of higher level students.

In addition to the structured activities, suggestions for open-ended activities are given in the Additional Activities section. These include role plays, debates and group work. The teacher can add specifications to the activity to fit the time and facilities available. For example, the teacher can determine the number of items that a group must list or the exact situation and length of a role play dialogue. While teachers will be familiar with most of the types of activities suggested, different ways of structuring the activities are given in the Instructor's Manual.

Additional Vocabulary

A section on additional vocabulary follows the structured activity. This section offers words and expressions related to the topic of the unit that may be of use to the students in the discussion and activities at the end of the unit. The teacher is free to omit or add to the vocabulary items.

Discussion Topics

A wide variety of discussion topics is given for each unit. Again, the teacher can choose the topics particularly relevant to the class. They function simply as conversation starters. Some bring up controversial issues; others simply invite the students to share their own experiences. The goal is that students talk about matters that interest them, and not that they try to answer every question posed in the section.

Assignments

Suggested assignments at the end of each unit give students the opportunity to pursue some of the topics on their own. The assignments require the students to try out what they have learned in actual conversation, to do independent research and to reflect on the material studied and their own experiences.

Instructor's Manual

An accompanying teacher's manual to *Take Part* offers many practical suggestions. The manual contains teaching strategies and hints on adapting the material to particular classes.

Cassette

A cassette audio tape is available to accompany *Take Part*. The tape includes all the dialogues from the text, as well as the news and weather reports and commercials. In addition, some of the pronunciation-based language notes are found on the tape.

ACKNOWLEDGEMENTS

The first edition of this text was class-tested at the English Language Program, Faculty of Extension, University of Alberta. We would like to thank the staff and students, especially Isabel Kent Henderson, Simone Devlin, Rosalie Banko and Ruth Pearce for their invaluable help.

The work of the staff at Prentice-Hall Canada is greatly appreciated. We would especially like to acknowledge the work of Monica Schwalbe, Marta Tomins and Terry Woo on the first edition. For their work on the second edition we would like to thank Elynor Kagan, Linda Gorman and Marjorie Walker.

The reviewers' comments on the manuscript proved especially helpful. The first edition was reviewed by Gail Gaffney, David Levy and Patricia Raymond. Additional material for the second edition was reviewed by Patricia Conway (Vanier College), Floyd Heneberry (Holy Name School), Patricia Parsons (Seneca College) and Avril Taylor (Mohawk College).

A very special thank-you goes to Garry Engkent and Ken Coomber for their contributions and support.

Getting Acquainted

The New Co-Worker

A new employee often gets an orientation tour of his or her workplace on the first day of the job. An important part of this tour is meeting fellow employees.

People often have difficulty remembering someone's name after an introduction. Repeating the name, as Susan does here, is a good technique to help learn names.

take over a job fill a position after someone has left it

how do you do an expression that is used to acknowledge an introduction (note that it is not a question)

show someone around take someone on a tour, act as a guide

PC personal computer

clunker (slang) old machine that does not work well

co-worker colleague, fellow worker

give you a hand (colloquial) help you

get the hang of it (colloquial) learn how to do something; get used to it

Terry:	Mrs. Dasko, do you have a minute?
Jane:	Certainly, Terry.
Terry:	I just wanted you to meet Susan Peterson. She'll be **taking over** Jeffrey's old job. Susan, this is Jane Dasko, the head of our accounting division.
Susan:	Pleased to meet you, Mrs. Dasko.
Jane:	**How do you do**. Did you start today?
Susan:	Yes, I did. Terry has been kind enough to **show me around** the office.
Jane:	I'm sure you'll like it here...
Terry:	And your desk is over here. This **PC** is a bit of a **clunker** but we're supposed to get new models soon. Eric, meet your new **co-worker** Susan Peterson. Susan, this is Eric McKee.
Eric:	Hi.
Susan:	Hi, Eric.
Terry:	Eric can **give you a hand** with any of the software packages that are different from those you were using at Gowans'.
Susan:	Great. But I'm sure it won't take me long to **get the hang of it**.
Eric:	No, this stuff is pretty straightforward. But when I was starting out here we had this old machine which was so much trouble...
Terry:	Oh no, if Eric is going to start reminiscing, I think I'll just move along.
Susan:	(laughs) Thanks for all your help, Terry.
Terry:	Don't mention it.

Discussion

1. Why is the first introduction in the dialogue more formal than the second?

2. What do you find different about the way Canadians greet people and introduce each other from the way people do so in your culture?

3. Are you good at remembering names and faces? What are some good ways to remember someone's name after an introduction?

Tenant Talk

There are many situations where people strike up an acquaintance with one another and have conversations, yet do not know each other's names. For example, two people may frequently see each other at a bus stop and exchange comments about the weather or make other small talk. It may be difficult to decide when and how to introduce themselves.

In the following situation, the two men live in the same apartment building. They have probably seen each other frequently and have exchanged casual words. In this conversation, this "nodding acquaintance" (a situation where you know someone by sight) progresses to a more social acquaintance. Because the men make a decision to go jogging together, their relationship changes and they need to exchange names. Notice that the best way to find out someone else's name is usually to offer your own name first.

Tenant 1:	(looking into his mailbox) **Hmmph!** Empty again!
Tenant 2:	Better than what I have — bills and more bills.
Tenant 1:	Depressing, **eh?**
Tenant 2:	Hey, did you hear the talk about rent increases?
Tenant 1:	What, again?
Tenant 2:	That's how it goes. The landlords have the **upper hand** right now because of the low **vacancy rate**.
Tenant 1:	Yeah, and even if you can find another place, with the cost of moving and all, it's better to **stay put**.
Tenant 2:	Trapped like rats in a cage.... Maybe a couple of laps around the track'll make me feel better.
Tenant 1:	You jog?
Tenant 2:	Yeah. I'm off to the field house now.
Tenant 1:	Where's that? I've been looking for an indoor track for weather like this.
Tenant 2:	It's at the sports centre on Main. You don't need a membership. You **wanna** come along and try it out?
Tenant 1:	Sure — I could use some exercise. Hey, by the way, my name's Craig McLeod.
Tenant 2:	(shaking hands) Hiroshi Nakamura. Why don't you go grab your **gear** and I'll meet you out front?
Tenant 1:	Great, I'll just be a second.

Hmmph! exclamation of disgust

eh interjection considered characteristic of Canadian English

upper hand the advantage, the better position

vacancy rate percentage of rental accommodations that are empty

stay put (colloquial) stay in one place

wanna spoken contraction of "want to"

gear equipment

Discussion

1. How is this introduction different from those in "The New Co-Worker"?

2. Discuss situations where you have had a nodding acquaintance with someone. Did you later learn the person's name? If you had to introduce yourself, how did you do so?

Waiting for the Bus

Exchanging comments about the weather is a common form of small talk. The following dialogue is an example of a casual exchange between two people at a bus stop. Notice that the two people do not know each other's names and yet do not introduce themselves in this conversation.

Cold enough for you?
(rhetorical question) implies that it is indeed very cold and that no one would want it any colder

pay hike increase in wages or salary, from the verb "to hike," meaning to raise

Stranger 1:	**Cold enough for you?**
Stranger 2:	Sure is. Can't get much colder.
Stranger 1:	At least the buses are running again.
Stranger 2:	(looks at his watch) Running late, you mean.
Stranger 1:	That **pay hike** the drivers got sure hasn't improved service.
Stranger 2:	Ah, here it comes now.

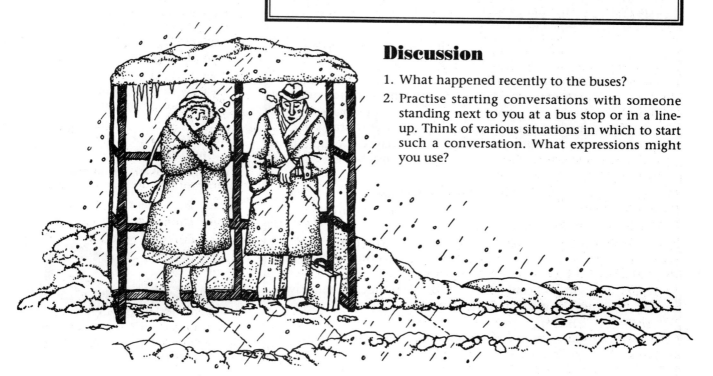

Discussion

1. What happened recently to the buses?
2. Practise starting conversations with someone standing next to you at a bus stop or in a line-up. Think of various situations in which to start such a conversation. What expressions might you use?

LANGUAGE NOTES

CONTRACTIONS

Contractions are used in informal standard English. The uncontracted forms are used in writing, in very formal speech, and for emphasis in spoken English. "I cannot do it," for example, is more emphatic than "I can't do it."

In positive statements, contractions are made with the verb *to be* or with the auxiliary verbs *have, had, will,* and *would.*

> *to be*—I'm, you're, he's, she's, it's, we're, they're
> *to have*—I've, you've, he's, she's, it's, we've, they've
> *will*—I'll, you'll, he'll, she'll, it'll, we'll, they'll
> *had* and *would*—I'd, you'd, he'd, she'd, it'd, we'd, they'd

Note that the contractions for *had* and *would* are the same. The same contracted form is also used for the third person singular of *to be* and *to have.* However, these contractions are followed by different forms of the main verb, so there is no confusion as to which auxiliary is meant.

> After I'd seen him, I found the book. (had)
> I'd go there if I could. (would)
> She's been here before. (has)
> She's working very hard. (is)

In conversational English, contractions can also be made with nouns.

> The doctor'll be here soon.
> John's going to be late again.

Non-native speakers often find contractions difficult to pronounce and many simply avoid using these forms. While it is not necessary to use contractions (except in some cases, such as tag questions), it is important to realize how they are pronounced.

Contractions reduce the sound of the verb so much that is often indistinguishable. In a form such as "I'd better," the contracted verb form sometimes drops entirely and the phrase sounds like "I better." Moreover, the "have" in contractions of "should have" and "could have" sounds like "of"; in fact, people often make a mistake and write "should of."

The pronoun is pronounced together with the contracted verb form as one word. Try pronouncing the following pairs of words. They should rhyme.

I'm—time	I'll—mile
you're—sure	you'll—tool
he's, she's—please	he'll, she'll, we'll—feel
it's—bits	it'll—little
we're—fear	they'll—fail
they're—there	I'd—ride
I've—five	you'd—rude
you've—move	he'd, she'd, we'd—feed
we've—leave	it'd—fitted
they've—save	they'd—made

TO GET

The verb *to get* is one of the most frequently used verbs in informal, spoken English. (Over-use of the verb should be avoided in writing.) Here are the main uses:

to receive, obtain
> That pay hike the drivers got sure hasn't improved service.
> He got a new car last week.
> I just got a letter from my friend in Yellowknife.

to become
> Can't get much colder.
> David got sick after the trip.
> He's always looking for a way to get rich quick.

to arrive at, reach
> How do you get to the Confederation Centre?
> I had so much other work to do that I couldn't get to that report.

to have (with the contraction of "have"; informal)
> You've got five minutes to catch that bus.
> I've got to go now.
> Susan's got a new job.

with prepositions forming two-word verbs
> You'll *get along* fine here. (do, manage, succeed)
> He *got up* late this morning. (arose, got out of bed)
> I don't know what you're *getting at*. (suggesting, saying in an indirect way)

There are many idiomatic expressions formed with the verb *to get* and prepositions. These are often difficult to learn, especially since each two-word verb formed may have several different meanings. For example:

> If you want to *get on* in the world, you'll have to dress well. (succeed, make progress)
> Wait till I *get* my coat *on*. (put on)
> It's *getting on* so I'd better go. (becoming late)

CULTURE NOTE

Generally, Canadians are informal and polite in their conversations. The rules for casual politeness vary with the social situation, but a few basic suggestions may be helpful.

Canadians prefer to be on a first-name basis with acquaintances. However, a title (such as Mr., Mrs., Miss or Ms.) with a last name is used when a person is addressing an employer, a teacher, a client, an older person, or a stranger in formal situations. First-name basis is often suggested by the person with more authority ("Call me Bob"). In Canada, first names are used less frequently than in the United States, and more frequently than in Britain. Calling someone by a last name without a title, however, is more common in Britain than in North America, where it is considered too abrupt. Here a last name alone can be used as a term of reference, not address. For example, we are more likely to say "Why don't you talk to Johnson about it?" than "I was wondering if you could help me with something, Johnson."

Calling a man "Sir," or a woman "Miss" or "Ma'am," is only done in certain circumstances. Salesclerks, waiters and others who serve the public will address customers in this way. These forms are also used to get someone's attention ("Excuse me, sir. You dropped your hat."). They are traditional terms of respect but are generally used less frequently today.

When introductions take place, shaking hands is customary, but much depends on the formality of the situation and individual preference. Handshakes are firm and brief. In conversations, Canadians generally do not touch each other as casually and frequently as people in other cultures do.

Canadians also prefer a greater distance between each other in conversation than that found in some other cultures. Here, a conversational distance of about one metre is quite acceptable. Any closer than this, and people may feel uncomfortable and uneasy. Of course, people who are intimate, such as close family members or lovers, will talk closer to one another.

Eye contact is another important factor in conversation. Looking away may be considered a sign of dishonesty, boredom or poor manners. On the other hand, staring, or looking too intently, may make a person feel uncomfortable.

In casual conversation, many Canadians also tend to avoid direct personal questions. Often such questions are phrased indirectly or vaguely (for instance, "Do you live around here?" instead of "Where do you live?").

Usually, when a subject of a personal nature is brought up, information is volunteered rather than asked for directly. In Canada, questions that can be considered too personal are those concerning age, religion, personal political beliefs, salary and prices paid for items. When personal questions are asked, they are phrased very carefully. For instance, someone might say, "Would you mind very much if I asked you how much you paid for that briefcase? I've been looking for one like that."

The guidelines for social situations are often difficult to learn. There are no written rules and the different factors of each situation must be taken into account. The degree of formality often varies. Moreover, some people are naturally more formal in manner, while others are more casual. Careful observation of native speakers is often the best way to learn how language is used.

MEET THE CLASS

Get to know the students in the class. Introduce yourself and make small talk. Try to answer the following questions with a different student's name for each one. Answer as many questions as you can and be sure to meet everyone in the class.

1. Who comes from the same country as you do?
2. Who has a pet?
3. Who plays a musical instrument?
4. Who takes public transit to come to school?
5. Who has studied ESL at another school in Canada?
6. Who has the same hobby as you do?
7. Who has lived in the area for less than three months?
8. Who likes to skate or ski?
9. Who lives close to you?
10. Who reads the newspaper every day?
11. Who would like to be a teacher?
12. Who has children?
13. Who listens to the radio on the way to school or work?
14. Who loves to cook?
15. Who likes to eat pizza?
16. Who speaks French?
17. Who plays tennis?
18. Who has been living in the area for more than two years?
19. Who likes to watch game shows on television?
20. Who owns a computer?

Now, do you remember who all the students are? Can you match names and faces? Use the information you have collected as the basis for further conversation. For example, if you have discovered that someone lives near you, you may wish to discuss different ways or routes of getting to the school.

Additional Vocabulary

chat   (informal) friendly informal conversation (also used as a verb)

conversation piece   object that serves as a topic of conversation because it is unusual

have the gift of the gab   have the ability to speak well continuously

gossip   talk about someone's private life, which may not be correct or proper (also used as a verb)

ice-breaker   topic or activity with which to start a conversation; something to "break the ice" between strangers

shop talk   conversation about job-related topics in a social situation

small talk   light talk or conversation between casual acquaintances

Informal Greetings

Hi. How are you?
How's it going?
What's new?
What've you been up to?

Types of Language

colloquialism   expression used in informal conversation (e.g., "kids" for children)

idiom   expression that has a different figurative meaning from its literal one (e.g. "shoot the breeze" for have a light conversation)

slang   language that is very informal and usually not acceptable in serious forms of writing or speaking; often slang terms belong to certain groups of people (such as teenagers) and go in and out of fashion quickly (e.g., "bread," "dough" or "bucks" for money)

Discussion Topics

1. Discuss your own observations about small talk among Canadians. Where, when and how do Canadians usually start a conversation? What do they talk about?

2. What topics might you discuss at a party? What topics would it be best to avoid?

3. What do you think is a good way to meet people?

4. In a group, how would you draw out someone who is shy? What questions might you ask to start a conversation?

5. What expressions do you often hear in casual conversations, greetings and introductions?

Additional Activities

1. In small groups, make a list of what all or most of the students in the group have in common.

2. In pairs, get to know a fellow classmate and then introduce your partner to the rest of the class.

3. In small groups, meet your classmates and exchange basic personal information. Change groups often in order to give everyone a chance to meet.

4. Think of situations in which you have had difficulty talking to someone at a first meeting. In small groups, discuss these situations and try to come up with some suggestions for dealing with them.

5. Role play conversations similar to those found in the dialogues in this unit.

Assignments

1. Start a friendly conversation with someone you don't know very well and report to the class on your experience.

2. Make a list of differences that are apparent in casual conversations of different cultures.

3. Identify conversational taboos of various cultures. It is a conversational taboo in Canada, for example, to inquire about an individual's salary.

Weather Watch

Winter Wear

Canadian winters can be an ordeal even for Canadians. Newcomers often have trouble acclimatizing to the snow and cold weather. However, being properly prepared for winter can mean the difference between suffering through the season or enjoying the pleasures it offers.

The following dialogue takes place as two friends enter a shopping mall.

no wonder (idiomatic) it's not surprising

hit (colloquial) reached, arrived at

balmy mild, warm

putting off delaying

get a move on (colloquial) be quick, hurry up

down-filled filled with soft, fluffy feathers (down) from waterfowl (ducks, geese)

parka a hip-length heavy coat with a hood, first worn in arctic regions

decked out (slang) dressed up

tuque (also spelled "toque") knitted, close-fitting hat without a brim

mukluks arctic-type boots with no heel

take something lightly (idiomatic) treat something as not serious

---

Adar: Brrrr. It's cold out there!

Hector: Yeah, but **no wonder** you're cold. That sweater doesn't look heavy enough for this weather.

Adar: It's not too bad. It hasn't been as cold as I expected.

Hector: We haven't really **hit** winter yet. Wait till January — this is practically **balmy**.

Adar: You're right. I've been **putting off** getting a winter coat and some boots, but I guess I'd better **get a move on**.

Hector: There's a sale on in that store. Let's take a look.

Adar: How about something like this ski jacket?

Hector: I dunno. I kinda like these **down-filled parkas**. They look bulky but they're quite light. I wish I'd gotten something like this myself — I always end up with several sweaters under my coat.

Adar: (trying a parka on) You're right. This is pretty neat. Hey, I should send home a picture of myself **decked out** in this winter gear.

Hector: (laughs) Well, if you're aiming for a Canadian image — don't forget the **tuque** and the **mukluks**.

Adar: All that?

Hector: (laughs) Those are just the basics.

Adar: I guess you can't **take winter lightly** here!

Discussion

1. Describe Adar and Hector. Do you think they are young or old? What is the relationship between them? Where do you think they are from?

2. Modify the dialogue so that two people in a shopping mall are discussing the purchase of other winter clothing or equipment (e.g., skis, snow tires, children's snowsuits, fur coat, sled, skates, snowmobile). Role play the new dialogue for the class.

3. What advice would you give someone preparing for his or her first winter in Canada?

4. The words for clothing items in English come from different sources. "Tuque," "parka" and "mukluks" are Canadian words derived from French and Aboriginal languages. In small groups, make lists of words for clothing that have come from different languages (like "sari" and "kimono") or lists of clothing for different seasons and weather conditions.

The Greenhouse Effect

Canadians' natural interest in the weather includes concerns about climatic change. The greenhouse effect has become a major environmental issue. Scientists think that air pollution and the destruction of forests have created higher levels of carbon dioxide in the earth's atmosphere, destroying the ozone layer which serves as the planet's cooling system. It is predicted that even a small increase in average temperatures will cause fertile areas to become deserts and polar ice to melt, raising the sea level and flooding many coastal areas.

The following dialogue is set on the beach.

Natasha: Want some **sunblock**?

Jessie: No, thanks, I'm going to sit over there in the shade as soon as I dry off. Too much sun and I'm all freckles and red blotches. You're lucky you're a **brunette**.

Natasha: True, but I don't try to get a suntan either. I've heard too many of those **doom and gloom** stories about the rise in skin cancer.

Jessie: Oh, you mean that stuff about the effects of the sun being worse now because of the thinning ozone layer.

Natasha: That's right. The greenhouse effect. Trouble is, **they** can't seem to agree on what it all means. **One guy says** it's normal for the earth's temperature to change over time; another guy says we're destroying our atmosphere. And some point out that a warmer climate for Canada does have advantages.

Jessie: But imagine all the polar ice melting and the higher sea level. Why, **P.E.I.** would practically disappear under water!

Natasha: Just the thought of all that beachfront real estate disappearing **is enough to give me nightmares**.

Jessie: That figures. That's all you **real estate agents** ever think about!

sunblock a cream or lotion to protect the skin from the harmful rays of the sun

brunette person who has brown hair

doom and gloom bad news, pessimism

they the pronoun is often used without a noun antecedent to refer generally to experts and news reporters, especially in the expression "they say"

one guy says informal way of reporting what experts have said; does not necessarily refer to a male

P.E.I. Prince Edward Island

is enough to give me nightmares worries me

real estate agents people who act as agents for buyers and sellers of houses and property

Discussion

1. Why do Jessie and Natasha not want to sit in the sun and tan?

2. How does Jessie joke about Natasha's fears about the greenhouse effect?

3. Discuss what you know about the greenhouse effect. Are you worried? What do you think should be done?

4. Find news stories about the greenhouse effect, its causes and its impact, and discuss them in class.

Weather Reports

Listening to the weather report on the radio or watching it on television is a ritual in most Canadians' lives. The weather in Canada is so changeable that people like to be forewarned, even if the forecasts are not always accurate.

take heart (idiomatic) be encouraged, cheer up

picnickers people going on a picnic

heat wave long period of very hot weather

record temperature highest or lowest temperature recorded for that day

nose dive (colloquial) sudden, sharp drop

Indian summer period of mild weather that occurs in the fall, after the first frost

traveller's advisory warning to travellers

pile-up a collision involving several cars

sanding operations icy roads are covered with sand to improve traction

"**Take heart**, all you golfers and **picnickers** — the rain is not here to stay. We can expect clearing skies tomorrow and a warm and sunny weekend. Highs should be around 26 degrees with lows near 16."

"There's no relief in sight from the hot, humid weather. Day 9 of the **heat wave** resulted in another **record temperature**. The record of 33 degrees for July 17 in 1943 was broken by today's high of 34. Local stores are reportedly unable to keep up with the demand for fans and air conditioners."

"Temperatures took a sharp **nose dive** last night and it looks like the end of the **Indian summer** we've been enjoying. There is a frost warning tonight as we expect even cooler temperatures. Low tonight: –2; high Wednesday: 10 degrees."

"The weather office has issued a **traveller's advisory** today as the freezing rain makes driving conditions hazardous. A six-car **pile-up** has closed Highway 2 southbound 50 kilometres from the city. **Sanding operations** are continuing and work crews are expected to be out all night. If you must be on the roads, be extremely careful."

Discussion

1. Which seasons do the weather reports describe? Describe the weather at the time of the reports in your own words.
2. Listen to radio or TV weather reports in class. Summarize the reports and list the weather vocabulary used.
3. In small groups, compose brief weather reports for different times of the year. Perform these reports for the class.
4. Compare the weather at various times of year in your native country with that in Canada. Discuss the differences with the class.

LANGUAGE NOTES

NEGATIVE CONTRACTIONS

Auxiliary verbs are often contracted with *not* in speech. The verb *to be* has two possible contractions with *not* ("he isn't," "he's not") for all persons except the first person singular. For the auxiliaries *have, will, would* and *had*, it is preferable to use the auxiliary contracted with *not* rather than the auxiliary contracted with the pronoun ("I haven't" rather than "I've not").

> *to be* — aren't, isn't (there is no contraction for *am* with *not*; "aren't I" is the form used in questions. "I'm not" is the only other form used)
> *to be* (past) — wasn't, weren't
> *to have* — haven't, hasn't
> *to do* — don't, doesn't

The following forms of auxiliary verb + *not* remain the same for each person:

> will not — won't
> did not — didn't
> had not — hadn't
> would not — wouldn't
> should not — shouldn't
> could not — couldn't
> cannot — can't
> must not — mustn't

The forms *needn't, oughtn't* and *mightn't* also exist but are not usually used in Canadian English.

Negative contractions are pronounced with no vowel sounds between the final sound of the verb, the *n* and the *t*. Some of the resulting consonant clusters are difficult for non-native speakers to pronounce. The nasal sound of the *n* should provide the bridge between a final consonant of the verb and the *t*.

Practise pronouncing the contractions in the dialogues and in the following sentences:

1. Don't worry, we won't be late.
2. I don't think it'll be warm tomorrow.
3. You'd better not take your winter tires off yet.
4. She doesn't mind if it's not sunny.
5. I can't go out without my umbrella.
6. It isn't raining that hard!
7. He wouldn't've been late if he'd had the car.
8. I haven't had a chance to finish that yet.
9. We weren't expecting company.
10. He wasn't back yet so I couldn't go.

STRESS OF AUXILIARY VERBS

Auxiliary verbs are not usually stressed in English, except for emphasis. Vowel sounds in unstressed syllables are reduced; they often become the sound "schwa" /ə/ or drop entirely. *Can*, for example, is often pronounced /kn/ in a sentence. However, auxiliary verbs with negative contractions do receive a stress. This stress pattern serves to signal the negative form. Improper stress on the auxiliary verb can result in a misunderstanding as to whether the positive or negative is meant, especially for the forms of *can*.

> I *can* go. (the auxiliary is pronounced /kn/ and the pitch rises on the main verb)
> I *can't* go. (the auxiliary is pronounced /kæn/ and the pitch rises on the auxiliary verb)

WEATHER-INSPIRED IDIOMS

While many idioms and expressions are used to describe weather conditions, weather-related terms are also used in other idioms.

> I didn't go to the party Saturday. I was feeling a bit *under the weather*. (not well)
> The recession was short-lived but many companies did not manage *to weather the storm*. (to pass safely through difficult times)
> Politicians are always accused of *being full of hot air*. (making false promises)
> My mother accepted the latest accident philosophically; she said, "*It never rains but it pours*." (misfortunes rarely come alone — a proverb)
> We could get together sometime and *shoot the breeze*. (chat, talk about unimportant matters)
> I didn't expect an income tax refund, so the money is a *windfall*. (unexpected lucky gift)
> She's been very secretive about that project — I have the feeling there's some change *in the wind*. (about to happen)
> He has *a snowball's chance in hell* of winning the election. (no chance at all)
> I can't take time off now — I'm really *snowed under* at work. (loaded heavily with things to do)
> It just goes to show that there's nothing new *under the sun*. (in the world)

CULTURE NOTE

Weather is probably one of the most popular topics for small talk among Canadians. After all, it's a neutral topic and, therefore, safe for conversation with people you do not know well. Canadian weather is so changeable, from season to season and from day to day, that there is always something that can be said about it. There are also many climatic differences among the various regions of Canada. When it is a mild, wet day in Vancouver, it can be -20 degrees and snowing in Manitoba.

Weather conditions have been shown to influence health and state of mind. For example, many Canadians suffer from the January or February "blahs," a feeling of mild depression. In fact, some people think that climate influences the personality of a people. A common stereotype is that people from northern climates are cold and unfriendly and that people from southern regions are hot-tempered and passionate.

Many people in the world think of Canada as simply a land of cold and snow; they are unprepared for the extremes of weather that Canadians experience. There are hot summers as well as cold winters. Many Canadians take pride in their ability to cope with adverse weather conditions.

Even so, Canadians grumble about the weather, especially the winter. Winter vacations in warm southern climates are popular, and many retired Canadians spend the winter in places like Florida and Arizona, largely for health reasons. Living in a country with distinct seasons has advantages, however. Most Canadians enjoy the all-too-brief summer and the incredibly beautiful autumn; they hope for a white Christmas and feel the joy of each new spring.

WEATHER IN CANADA

Look at the weather facts about different Canadian cities given on the next page. Identify the cities on the map of Canada. In small groups, compare the cities. Compare the area of Canada in which you live to others. What are the warmest and coldest regions of the country? Which areas get more precipitation? Discuss which cities you would like to live in and which you would not.

The temperatures in the chart are in degrees Celsius. Notice that the total precipitation (rain and snow) is given in millimetres, while the total snowfall is given in centimetres.

"C.S.I." refers to the Climate Severity Index, which rates the weather of Canadian cities on a scale of 1 to 100. A score of 1 represents the least severe climate and a score of 100 represents the worst.

| | MEAN TEMPERATURE (°C) | | PRECIPITATION | | |
	JANUARY	JULY	TOTAL/mm	SNOW/cm	C.S.I.
Calgary	–12	16	405	72	35
Charlottetown	–7	18	1256	330	48
Edmonton	–15	17	531	54	43
Fredericton	–9	19	1011	228	41
Halifax	–3	18	1546	134	47
Montreal	–9	22	803	174	43
Ottawa	–11	21	869	187	44
Quebec City	–12	19	1053	308	52
Regina	–18	19	306	78	49
St. John's	–4	16	1508	243	59
Toronto	–7	21	647	94	36
Vancouver	3	17	1252	9	19
Victoria	4	15	823	2	15
Whitehorse	–21	14	336	114	46
Winnipeg	–19	20	380	110	51
Yellowknife	–29	16	267	135	57

Additional Vocabulary

blizzard   severe snowstorm

hail   rounded lumps of ice that may fall during thunderstorms

downpour   heavy rainfall

drizzle   very light rainfall

chilly   rather cold, unpleasantly cold

wind-chill factor   the chilling effect of wind in combination with low temperatures

slush   partly melted, wet snow

to winterize   to prepare (usually a car or a building) for winter

drifting snow   snow that is blown about and heaped up by the wind

it's raining cats and dogs   (idiomatic) it's raining very hard

acid rain   rain that is acidic because of air pollution and causes damage to lakes and plant life

Discussion Topics

1. How do you think the weather affects people?
2. Do you think different cultures have different personalities because of climate?
3. What would be the ideal climate for you?
4. What is your cure for mid-winter depression?
5. Which season or month is do you enjoy most? Why?

Additional Activities

1. With the aid of a map, role play a national TV weather report.
2. In pairs, develop and role play a dialogue about the weather of the day.
3. In groups, discuss environmental problems such as the greenhouse effect and acid rain, and determine what you think should be done by government, business and private citizens.

Assignments

1. Keep track of the number of times people start conversations with small talk about the weather. Keep a record of different expressions. Report to the class any interesting findings.
2. Make a list of weather terms not included in the vocabulary lists.

3

The Workplace

Telecommuting

Technological advances in computers and communications have made the home office a reality. Some people have their own home-based businesses while others telecommute to the office.

I'll say I agree, that's true

workaholic someone addicted to work

thing situation (the use of vague terms like "thing" in this manner is characteristic of informal English)

telecommuting reaching the workplace through use of telephone lines rather than actually travelling there

fed up unhappy, tired

fax machine that sends copies of documents or pictures over the phone lines

modem machine that transmits a computer's signals over a phone line to another computer

touch base make contact with someone, find out what someone is doing

give someone a hard time make life difficult for someone, argue with someone

keeps track follows

maternity leave time off work to have a baby (time can range from a few weeks to a few months and pay arrangements also vary)

go for it agree to it

Grace: I'll be glad when this report is finally finished and we quit working all this overtime.

Farid: **I'll say.** I've missed too many of my daughter's soccer games as is.

Grace: Good thing this only happens once in a while. One reason I left my old job was because the department head was such a **workaholic** that we all had to put in 60-hour weeks to keep up with her.

Farid: Yeah, I know the type. Try taking time off for a family **thing** and it's like you're a traitor to the organization.

Grace: You know, I've been wondering about this set-up that Alan has.

Farid: You mean the **telecommuting?**

Grace: Yeah. What do you know about it?

Farid: Well, let's see. Alan got **fed up** with driving in from Barrie every day, so he asked Vlad if he could set up his computer at home. He uses the telephone, a **fax** and a **modem,** but he still comes into the office once or twice a week for meetings and to **touch base** with everyone.

Grace: And did Vlad **give him a hard time** when he suggested this? I mean, isn't it hard to supervise an employee who is 50 km away?

Farid: Nah. Vlad **keeps track** of the work Alan is doing by what is being sent in to our computer and Vlad is just as happy to free up some office space here. Alan says he actually gets more work done without the distractions here and without the stress of the commute added to his day.

Grace: Sounds like a good deal. I've been thinking of approaching Vlad for an arrangement like that myself. I'll be off on **maternity leave** soon, but I don't really want to come back here full time.

Farid: Won't it be hard to keep up with the work and take care of the baby?

Grace: I was thinking of taking on a lighter work load — the reduced income won't matter too much if I'm saving on child-care expenses. And Geoff's schedule is flexible, so between the two of us we should be able to take care of the baby and keep our jobs.

Farid: Sounds like a good idea. I'm sure Vlad will **go for it.**

Discussion

1. Why is Grace interested in what Alan is doing?
2. What are the advantages and disadvantages of telecommuting?

3. In small groups, make lists of the types of jobs that one could easily do at home and jobs that could not be home-based.

The Job Interview

Job interviews are unusual types of conversations because they are not really exchanges of information: the interviewer often has much of the information available in the job application or résumé. The job candidate is asked to expand upon or explain some of the information, but the interview is really more an opportunity to find out how well the candidate presents himself or herself.

Although the dialogue below is shorter than the usual interview, several of the techniques shown are common to the job interview situation. For example, the interviewee should explain and offer information, rather than just giving "yes" and "no" responses. A team of interviewers often works together to ask questions and evaluate the prospective employee.

Mario: Ingrid Bekker? Please come in and sit down.

Ingrid: Thank you.

Mario: My name is Mario Baruzzi and this is Allison LeClair, the head of the museum's children's programmes division.

Ingrid: Pleased to meet you.

Mario: Before we begin, I'd like to go over a few particulars of the position. Your official title would be Museum **Interpreter**. Essentially, that means working in our **live history exhibits**, explaining the displays, and giving tours through the museum. Are you familiar with our **set-up**?

Ingrid: Oh, yes. I've seen the museum interpreters at work many times.

Mario: Fine. As you know, this is a part-time job, 10–15 hours a week. Many of our interpreters are students and we give them the opportunity to schedule their work hours around their class times. On your résumé, it says that you are a student at St. Laurent University. Could you tell us something about your studies?

Ingrid: Certainly. I'm majoring in history — early Canadian history, mostly. My interest in the pioneer settlements in Canada is what led me to apply for this job.

Allison: Most of the work you've done before seems to be research-oriented. How do you feel about working with the public, especially children?

Ingrid: I enjoy being with children—I come from a large family so I've done my share of babysitting. The chance to work with the public is an aspect of this job that really appeals to me.

Mario: When our interpreters work in the live history exhibits, they have to do the work of the pioneers and to dress in **period costume**. We do train them for the work, but they also have to have a certain aptitude. For the women, this means being able to handle various domestic chores.

continued

interpreter someone who explains the meaning of something

live history exhibits historical sites and museums often have displays showing life in the past — whole rooms and buildings with employees dressed in costume, doing various activities of everyday life of the time

set-up establishment, institution

period costume type of clothing worn in that historical period

churning butter making butter by beating milk

all thumbs clumsy

a mean hand at something (colloquialism) good at something

tackle deal with

Ingrid: My hobbies include needlework and weaving, and I've experimented with a number of pioneer tasks such as spinning, dipping candles and **churning butter**. I know how much skill goes into doing these jobs well, but I'm sure I won't be **all thumbs** when it comes to learning to do them in the museum. It's a shame the division of labour was so strict in those days, because I'm a **mean hand** at carpentry.

Allison: Well, it seems as if you are well-prepared to **tackle** the challenges of this job. Do you have any questions?

Ingrid: No, I don't think so.

Mario: Well, we do have a lot of applicants still to see. We should be able to let you know one way or the other sometime next week. Thank you for coming.

Ingrid: Thank you for taking the time to see me. Good-bye.

Discussion

1. How is the language of this dialogue more formal than the others you have read in this book?

2. Do you think Ingrid will get the job? Why or why not?

3. Make a list of various tasks that men and women had to do in pioneer days. Which tasks do you know how to do?

4. Role play a job interview for the class. In a class discussion, evaluate each interview. Would you give the job to the candidate? Why or why not?

5. In small groups, go through "Help Wanted" ads and pick out a few interesting positions. Discuss the qualifications and personal qualities that would be necessary for the job.

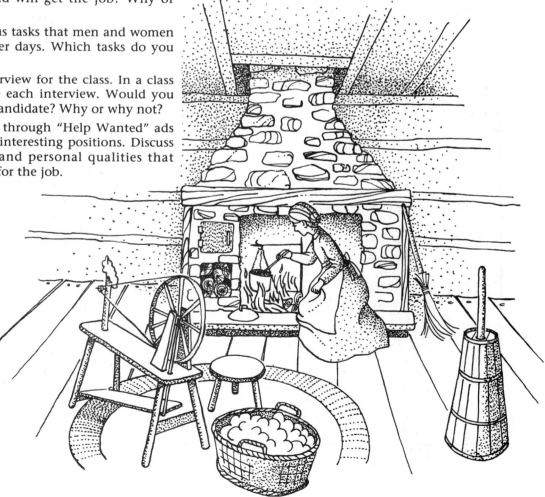

LANGUAGE NOTES

FORMAL AND INFORMAL ENGLISH

Different registers (levels) of a language are required in different situations, and the degree of formality may also vary according to the personal preferences of the individual speaker. Informal English is used in many everyday conversations and in friendly letters. Formal English is required in most writing and in more formal speaking situations, such as job interviews and speeches.

Formal spoken English is closer to written English in form and style. Sentences can be longer and more complex; words and pronunciation are more precise. Informal English, on the other hand, is characterized by the use of colloquialisms, slang, short forms, ellipsis (leaving words out) and incomplete sentences. Sounds are often reduced and contractions are used. Informality usually implies familiarity (in other words, we are less formal with people we know better). With people we know better, it is easier to take short cuts in language and still be understood.

Here are examples of some of the differences between informal and formal English:

Informal	Formal
Yeah	Yes
kids	children
pretty bad	quite bad
ten bucks	ten dollars
a lot of	many
I dunno	I don't know
stuff	objects, items

Change the informal English into more formal English in the following dialogue:

Interviewer: Good morning, Mr. O'Connor. How are you today?

Sean: Pretty good, I guess. How 'bout you?

Interviewer: Fine, thank you. The interview should only take half an hour. First of all we'd like you to write a short essay.

Sean: Yeah, sure. What about?

Interviewer: We'd like you to explain your views on the use of computers in this business.

Sean: You know, I don't know a lot about your business, but I'll give it a go, okay? Anyway, when it comes to computers — that's my thing. I know a lot about them.

Interviewer: Please take a seat here — I'll be back in 15 minutes.

Sean: You bet.

QUESTIONS OF GRAMMAR

Just as vocabulary and pronunciation change, so rules of grammar alter over the history of a language. Changes are usually found first in spoken, informal language and then move into more formal registers. In English, for example, the use of progressive (or continuous) tenses has increased; in Shakespeare's *Hamlet* (II.ii.191), Polonius asks, "What do you read, my lord?," whereas today he would be more likely to ask, "What are you reading?" In addition, some forms, such as the use of *whom* and the subjunctive ("If I *were* rich..."), are dying out.

In informal spoken English, a number of commonly used forms are generally considered ungrammatical. One is the use of *here's* and *there's* with plural subjects (probably because of ease of pronunciation):

> There's lots of supplies in the cupboard.
> Where's my boots?
> Here's the books you wanted.

Although *everybody* is singular, it is commonly used with a plural pronoun. This usage has probably arisen out of a need to get around the awkward "his or her" structure.

> Everybody take out their math books. It's time for the next lesson.
> Everyone wants their picture taken for the yearbook.

Pronoun usage causes many problems for English speakers. Although "It's me" has often been criticized as being ungrammatical, few people say "It is I" and the variation has become acceptable. However, the frequently used "between you and I," which is thought to have started as an over-correction, is a noticeable error.

Correctness of usage is a hotly debated topic and even language scholars have different opinions. For instance, some say that the use of "hopefully" to mean "I hope that" is incorrect, while others say that it is acceptable because it follows a pattern and fulfills a need in English. The fact that native speakers do not agree makes it even more difficult for language students to learn "good English." A good guideline to follow is that informal English allows much more of this type of grammatical flexibility and that formal English should be more "correct."

TALENT IDIOMS

Many idioms that describe different talents refer to parts of the body:

> She has a *head for figures.*
> Your daughter has a good *ear for music.*
> An interior designer must have a good *eye for colour.*
> A good reporter has a *nose for news.*
> He's very good with plants; he has a *green thumb.*

She never gives away what she is thinking — she has a real *poker face.*
He has a *silver tongue* — he can talk anyone into anything.

Similar idioms are used for a lack of talent:

> I can't dance — I have *two left feet.*
> He's *all thumbs* when it comes to anything mechanical.
> I'm not very good at music — I have a *tin ear.*

CULTURE NOTE

Changes in society have meant changes in fundamental attitudes towards work. The work ethic values labour for its own sake, with the belief that working hard is important, not only to earn enough money to live on, but to achieve success and satisfaction. People's occupations largely determine their status in society.

Increasingly, however, Canadians have found that they are working too hard. Although it was predicted that people would have more leisure time by the end of the twnetieth century, the opposite seems to be true — people are putting in longer hours today. In families where both parents hold full-time jobs, off-work hours are filled with household chores and parenting activities, leaving little time to relax and enjoy life.

It is not surprising that some people have decided that there is more to life than work. Some change their work habits —

bringing less work home, putting in fewer hours of overtime or even choosing part-time work or job-sharing. The demands of family life have been recognized in company benefits such as parental leave (for new parents or for parents whose children are ill), more flexibility in work hours and the opportunity to work from home.

Traditional values towards work are also being questioned. For example, corporate loyalty is no longer an important issue as people today rarely spend most of their working lives in one organization. Moreover, people may refuse promotions or transfers if the new positions do not fit in with their notions of the work they wish to do or where they wish to live.

Most workplace issues centre on the balance between human needs and the need to make money. Profit, of course, is essential to business, but human needs must be taken into account. Business must consider the general welfare of the work force, the safety of the environment and the general good of society. Canadians are concerned about these issues and "business ethics" is a much-debated topic.

Environmental issues often highlight the social responsibility of business. Pollution controls and recycling programmes are expensive, yet they can benefit a company. For example, consumers are increasingly attracted to "green" products. Moreover, caring for the environment is a long-term investment since it protects the resources the company must use and the world in which it must operate.

A skilled workforce is also a resource. Employers are recognizing the importance of workers' health and morale to productivity. Poor work conditions mean higher employee turnover, which in turn means higher costs for hiring and training. Therefore, many employers aim to provide good working conditions and benefits. Some have instituted programmes such as counselling services, fitness breaks and day-care facilities in the workplace.

WHO GETS PROMOTED?

Zachary Hightower is a manager in a medium-sized computer company, TechnoBits Inc. His assistant manager has just resigned because his wife is being transferred to another city. Hightower is trying to make a choice among several promising candidates for the vacant position. The job requires good leadership and organizational skills. Technical knowledge is not necessary, but familiarity with the product is helpful.

In small groups, consider the qualifications and characteristics of each of the candidates below. What do you think are the most important criteria for this hiring decision? Which factors do you feel are less important? You may wish to make a list of questions that Hightower should ask when he interviews the candidates. With your group, decide which person you think would be best suited to the job. You can also role play the job interviews, adding more information as necessary.

THE CANDIDATES

Drew Austin was hired as a management trainee after he completed his B.Sc. He has been working at TechnoBits for eight months in a senior clerical position. He is 24 years old and single. He is also Hightower's nephew. Austin is still learning the ropes at the company and has, therefore, not made much of an impression on his supervisor. She says that he is hard-working and conscientious, but that he lacks creativity and that his work is not outstanding. He is very quiet and has not yet made friends with his co-workers.

Amelia Jelinski is Zachary Hightower's executive secretary. She has been with the company for 20 years and has worked her way up from the typing pool. While she did not attend university, she did one year at a business college after high school, before coming to TechnoBits. Since then, Jelinski has taken many night courses in both business and computers. She is well liked by all the staff and keeps things running smoothly in the office. She is 40 years old, is married and has two teen-aged children.

Winona Ho has applied for the job from another company where she has worked in a position similar to the assistant manager's. She wants to leave the other company because she feels that TechnoBits will offer her more chance for promotion; she feels that she has hit the "glass ceiling" (the limit for promotions for women) at her company. Ho is 30 years old, is married and has no children. She is bright and ambitious. Hightower knows her boss, who says that Ho is a go-getter but sometimes steps on colleagues' toes. However, Hightower knows the boss is somewhat chauvinistic and does not like aggressive women.

Pierre Sauvé is an assistant manager in a small branch office of the company. He has been with the company for five years. He is 50 years old, is divorced and has three adult children. He is interested in this job because it would give him an opportunity to move to a larger city. His strong sales skills have made him successful in the branch office, but they would not be as important in the position at head office.

Additional Vocabulary

trade skilled mechanical work (e.g., machine technician)

profession occupation requiring special education and training (e.g., medicine or law)

salary fixed annual rate of pay usually for professional and office work (e.g., a salary of $20 000)

wage fixed hourly rate of pay usually for manual and physical work (e.g., a wage of $5.60 an hour)

white-collar office or sales work (where men traditionally wear a suit and tie), for which one is usually paid a salary

blue-collar manual and physical work for which one is usually paid a wage

résumé a brief account of one's career, qualifications and employment history

curriculum vitae (C.V.) (Latin) résumé for academic purposes, dealing more extensively with education

bottom line the result in a budget, the total figure giving profit or loss

Discussion Topics

1. If you could choose any occupation, which would you choose and why?

2. Do you believe "One works to live" or "One lives to work"? Explain the difference.

3. What advice would you give someone looking for a job?

4. What occupations do you feel are the most stressful?

5. How should the value or worth of a job be decided in order to determine salary? Rank some jobs in terms of their relative value. For example, should a teacher earn more than a plumber?

6. What social and environmental responsibilities does business have?

Additional Activities

1. In groups, act as employment counsellors for your classmates. Ask questions to determine each individual's interests and talents. Suggest training and education possibilities in order for the student to pursue the career you recommend.

2. In pairs, develop and role play a dialogue where a supervisor disciplines or fires an employee.

3. Make an oral presentation to the class about a job that you have had or would like to have.

4. In groups, review vocabulary by making a list of occupations.

Assignments

1. Visit a Canada Employment Centre and find out what kinds of jobs are available. Look through any available information giving advice to job-seekers.

2. Research information on how to write a job application letter and a résumé.

3. Look at various job application forms and compare the questions that are asked.

Leisure Time

Mystery Buffs

Movies, television and other entertainment activities are a common topic of casual conversation. People like to hear others' opinions on movies or shows, especially if they are looking for something to do on a night out. If you are asked for your opinion, it is important to give enough information, without spoiling the show.

pretty quiet (colloquial) fairly quiet

Agatha Christie whodunit a murder mystery by Agatha Christie; "whodunit" is from "who done (non-standard for "did") it?"; "it" refers to the murder

all-star cast cast of famous actors and actresses

eccentric odd, unusual

figure out solve the mystery or the problem

hunch idea based on feeling rather than reason

catch on understand, see the significance of

you (colloquial) people in general

play along join the game

the butler did it an old cliché of murder mysteries; butler is the chief male servant of a household

spill the beans (colloquial) reveal a secret

Ricardo: How was your weekend?

Carolyn: **Pretty quiet.** Just did a few things around the house. I spent Saturday night curled up in front of the fire with a book. Did you do anything interesting?

Ricardo: Jackie and I went to see the new movie at the Capitol.

Carolyn: Oh, yeah? Any good?

Ricardo: Not bad. It's an **Agatha Christie whodunit.**

Carolyn: Oh, I like those. **An all-star cast,** I suppose.

Ricardo: Yeah, all playing **eccentric** characters — the type you only ever see in murder mysteries.

Carolyn: Did you **figure out** who the murderer was?

Ricardo: I had a **hunch** but I didn't **catch on** to all the clues.

Carolyn: Did the detective call all the suspects together at the end?

Ricardo: Yeah, and he went over the clues and the possible motives, and just when it looked like they all could have done it, he revealed the murderer's identity.

Carolyn: Well, don't tell me who did it. I want to see that movie and it's no fun if **you** can't **play along.**

Ricardo: Okay, I won't tell you that **the butler did it.**

Carolyn: Rick!

Ricardo: Just kidding. There wasn't even a butler in the film.

Carolyn: Well, maybe I'd better get going before you really do **spill the beans.**

Ricardo: I should get back to work myself. Bye.

Carolyn: See you later.

Discussion

1. Where do you think this dialogue is taking place?
2. Who do you think Jackie is?
3. How does Ricardo tease Carolyn?
4. Develop and role play a dialogue starting with the question: "What did you do on the weekend?"
5. Do you read mystery novels or watch detective shows? Do you get involved in solving the mysteries? Tell your classmates about a mystery that you have read or watched.

Weekend Hobbies

Few people are fortunate enough to have jobs that give them a chance to pursue their interests. Hobbies and leisure-time activities allow people to develop new skills, be creative or unwind from work. Unfortunately, the time and money to pursue such interests seem to be in short supply in today's demanding world, so that, while many people do participate in leisure activities such as sports or travel, fewer have hobbies.

Chris: Thank goodness it's Friday. I've been looking forward to the weekend since Monday.

Anna: I thought you enjoyed your work.

Chris: Oh, I do. I mean, it's not that bad. But I'm not a **workaholic** or anything. I really appreciate my time off.

Anna: I don't like weekends. First I run around **like crazy** trying to get the housework done. Then I lie around and **veg** to try to recuperate for Monday.

Chris: Yeah, it's **rough**. I try to get most of my chores done on weeknights to leave the weekend free.

Anna: To do what?

Chris: Oh, different things. Right now **I'm really into** painting. I spend my Sundays in the country doing **landscapes**.

Anna: I didn't know you were an artist.

Chris: Calling my painting art is really **stretching it**. I just like to **dabble** in it. And I also try to get in some squash or tennis.

Anna: How do you find time for all of that?

Chris: Just takes a bit of organization. My leisure time is important to me — so I make time. And look at Greg — you know those **ceramic** pieces he's always making at home? Well, he sells them to a local **handicrafts** store. Fun *and* profit.

Anna: I'm afraid I'm **all thumbs** when it comes to things like that.

Chris: Do you have any hobbies?

Anna: Nothing I **stick to**. I used to play guitar when I was a kid. Last year I thought of **taking up** photography but the equipment can be so expensive.

Chris: But you could get into it gradually. No need to **go overboard** with fancy gadgets. You've got a pretty decent camera already and if you take a course at the community centre you'll have access to their darkroom facilities.

Anna: Hmmm, that's true. Maybe I'll look into a course to get me started.

---

workaholic (colloquial) non-stop worker, someone addicted to working

like crazy in a wild way

veg (slang) short form of "vegetate" — to be inactive, like a plant

rough (informal) difficult

I'm really into (slang) I'm extremely interested in

landscapes drawings and paintings of outdoor scenes

stretching it (colloquial) exaggerating

dabble play, do something for fun, not seriously

ceramic pottery, made of clay

handicrafts any art using the hands (e.g., pottery, weaving)

all thumbs clumsy

stick to keep doing

take up begin, start

go overboard go too far, be over-enthusiastic

Discussion

1. Where and when is this dialogue taking place?
2. Name and describe the leisure-time activities mentioned in the dialogue.
3. What are the characteristics of a workaholic?
4. What leisure-time activities do you enjoy most?

LANGUAGE NOTES

QUALIFIERS

In informal spoken English, there are a number of qualifiers that are used with adjectives. Some of these (such as *pretty* and *real*) are not used in formal English. The varying degrees of strength for these qualifiers can often be confusing.

a little, a little bit   weakest
kind of, sort of
pretty, quite, rather
real, really, terribly, awfully   strongest

Quite and *rather* are more common in British English. *Real* (instead of *really*) in front of an adjective is considered very informal, even slang. This use is more common in American English than Canadian English. *Pretty* is used frequently in spoken English.

Examples:

1. I'm kind of tired — maybe I should stay home tonight.
2. He's really glad to be going home; he hated it here.
3. It's quite far — maybe you should take a bus.
4. No, he won't be seeing a doctor; he's just a little under the weather.
5. I was awfully scared when I heard the siren so close.

Supply the missing qualifiers in the following dialogues:

1. *A:* How was your weekend?
   B: Horrible! I'm _____ exhausted. I was busy all weekend.
2. *A:* What did you think of the play?
   B: I thought it was _____ boring actually.
3. *A:* That magazine article was insulting.
   B: No kidding! It used every name-calling technique you could think of.
4. *A:* Chess is hard to learn, isn't it?
   B: _____ . Actually, it's _____ easy to learn, _____ difficult to master.
5. *A:* It was _____ cold out at the barbecue last week.
   B: That's for sure. I had to wear two sweaters and stay by the campfire.

NOUN COMPOUNDS

In English, nouns often function as adjectives to describe other nouns. The first noun, or the noun/adjective, specifically explains and describes the second noun, categorizing it:

a stamp album
an Agatha Christie mystery
a racquetball player

If other adjectives are used, they come before the noun/adjective:

an interesting detective story
the white-haired antique collector

Noun compounds are formed through the use of nouns as adjectives. Some noun compounds are written as two words, some are hyphenated, and others become one word.

cassette tape
tennis court
bus station

bottle-opener
stamp-collector
baby-food

bookcase
housework
raincoat

Make the following phrases into noun compounds where possible:

1. a computer for the home
2. a cup of water
3. tickets for the theatre
4. a bar of soap
5. a magazine for travel

Make the following noun compounds into noun phrases:

1. a bird house
2. a glass coffee table
3. a picture frame
4. a fountain pen
5. a coffee cup

CULTURE NOTE

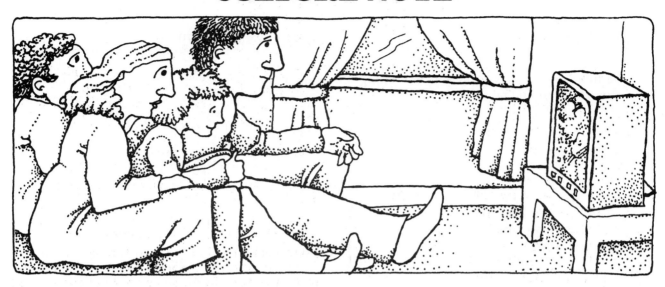

Watching television is the most popular leisure-time activity. Ninety-eight percent of Canadian homes have a TV set; two-thirds receive cable TV. While statistics report that we spend an average of 24 hours a week on television, it is difficult to say how much of this time is spent actually watching the programmes. Often television is combined with another activity such as housework or reading the newspaper, and some people have the TV on during the day as background noise, instead of a radio.

Although public television and pay-TV channels are available, North American television is dominated by commercial television, where programmes are interrupted by advertisements every eight minutes or so. Commercial networks get their revenue from advertisers based on how many viewers their programmes attract. Therefore, programmes have to appeal to a broad range of viewers or to a certain group the advertisers wish to target.

Remote control channel changers and video cassette recorders (VCRs) have changed the way people watch television.

People flip the channel during commercials or "zap" the ads by fast-forwarding through them when watching taped programmes. Advertisers, therefore, try to make the commercials more entertaining in an effort to hold people's attention.

Canadian television is dominated by programmes originating in the United States. Although the CRTC (Canadian Radio-television and Telecommunications Commission) demands Canadian content on the airwaves, most Canadians can receive a number of American channels. Moreover, it is more profitable for Canadian TV stations to purchase American programmes than to produce their own.

The overwhelming influence of American TV makes the country seem more American than it is. For example, Canadians who watch American police and detective programs learn about the American legal system and wrongly assume that Canada's laws are the same. Many Canadians can name more American presidents than Canadian prime ministers. While good Canadian programmes are being made, the laws of economics ensure the domination of American TV.

Television is a mirror of culture and many of the criticisms of TV reflect important social issues. For example, the stereotyping of ethnic minorities and women has come under fire. Moreover, many people feel that violence on TV encourages viewers to commit crimes in real life. In addition, many children's programmes favour a good guy/bad guy approach to the world that does little to teach important values such as acceptance and compromise. Controversies concerning the depiction of violence and sexual explicitness on television lead to debates on censorship.

Despite these disadvantages, television can be an important educational tool as well as a source of entertainment. Canadian television has a reputation for some of the world's best documentaries and public affairs programs. Cable services often carry local channels that broadcast university lectures and school plays. Some correspondence courses have televised lectures. Although Canadians often complain about television, there is enough choice to please almost everyone. Programs include religious shows, sports events, adventures and children's shows.

MURDER AT LOVESICK LAKE

The characters in the dialogue "Mystery Buffs" enjoy mystery films. Murder mystery evenings or weekends are popular leisure activities. In some, actors play roles while the guests try to figure out "whodunit"; in others, usually small parties, guests come as characters in the mystery.

   The following mystery gives you the setting, the main action and the characters. Explain what steps Inspector Cliché should take to solve the mystery. You can act out the mystery and its resolution with role plays. Or you can discuss the case in small group discussions. Each group can present its solution to the class and the class can vote to decide the "best" solution (e.g., most plausible or most creative).

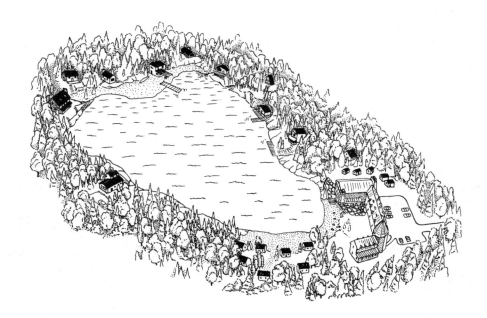

THE SETTING

Lovesick Lake is in Ontario's cottage country. Lovesick Lake Lodge is a popular resort at one end of the small lake. It has a main lodge building with guest rooms and several small cabins for rent. The remaining lakeshore is dotted with private summer cottages.

THE CHARACTERS

Professor Alan Summerville, the murder victim, was a professor of computer science at a prestigious Canadian university. He had also been developing computer programs for projects for the Canadian government. His colleagues considered him to be brilliant but overbearing. He had owned a cottage at Lovesick Lake for several years.

   Inspector Anne-Marie Cliché is a detective with the RCMP. She is from Regina but is staying at her grandparents' cottage at Lovesick Lake. She wants to solve the murder quickly before the homicide detachment arrives so that she can get the credit and perhaps a promotion.

Jack Malone is the owner of the Lovesick Lake Lodge. He has wanted to buy Professor Summerville's land for some years in order to expand the lodge area with more lakeside cabins. He was overheard to have had a loud argument with the professor the day before the murder. Malone is a veteran hunter who has hunting guns at the lodge.

   Mark Polanski is a graduate student of the professor's. He has just found out that the professor has sold a software package very similar to the one Polanski himself was working on. He has come to the lodge to confront the professor with stealing his work, but claims that he did not have a chance to talk to the professor privately.

   Audrey Summerville is the professor's ex-wife. She divorced him when she found out that he'd been having an affair with a graduate student. She is at the lake hoping to find out where the professor has hidden his money, since he claimed he was broke when the divorce proceedings were taking place. She is American and went back to live in the United States after the divorce.

Harry Niven is the caretaker at the lodge, and a former hunting guide. He rarely talks to other people but is often seen mumbling to himself. He often stares at people but is not known to have a personal grudge against the professor. Niven was under psychiatric care after attempting suicide; he claimed that he heard voices urging him to kill himself.

Miranda Chan is the professor's colleague from the computer science department. She and Summerville have been romantically involved for several months but they have been keeping their affair a secret from their co-workers. Chan wanted to publicize their relationship and hoped to marry the professor, but he resisted that idea. She has been staying at the cottage with him, but left the party before he did. Her hobby is target-shooting.

THE CRIME

On a Saturday evening in early September, a party was held at the lodge. All the characters attended, but not all at the same time. All left at different times. The professor's body was discovered lying near his cottage. He apparently was killed on his way home from the party. He had been shot at long range. The professor left the party when a thunderstorm was starting up. The storm brought down the power lines so the local authorities have not yet been notified. Thus, Inspector Cliché has no autopsy or ballistics report to help her. Guns would have been readily available to all the suspects.

Additional Vocabulary

cocooning   staying home for one's entertainment, perhaps with take-out food and rented movies.

couch potato   (slang) someone who watches a lot of television and engages in little activity.

censor   to edit or repress material, such as passages in a book or scenes in a movie, for political or moral reasons.

dub   to change the sound track, especially the voices, of a movie (e.g., foreign films playing in Canada sometimes have English-speaking actors saying the lines)

subtitles   the translated text of the film appearing in print at the bottom of the screen.

Different Genres of Movies and Books

mystery, thriller, suspense, detective story
horror
science fiction, fantasy
romance
comedy, humour
western
historical fiction
non-fiction, documentary
biography

Pastimes and Hobbies

card games (bridge, poker, gin, euchre, cribbage)
board games (chess, checkers, Monopoly, Scrabble)
trivia games
puzzles (jigsaws, crosswords)
collecting (coins, stamps, knick-knacks, souvenirs)
crafts (sewing, quilting, crocheting, woodwork, ceramics)
dancing (ballroom, disco, folk)
video games, computer games
birdwatching

Sports

fishing, hunting, camping
cycling, hiking, jogging, swimming
canoeing, sailing, surfing, skiing, skating
badminton, tennis, recquetball, squash, ping-pong, volleyball, basketball, football, soccer, baseball, hockey, lacrosse, golf, pool
martial arts (judo, karate)
gymnastics
weight-lifting, track, aerobics

Music

listening (rock, country 'n western, folk, jazz, classical, opera)
playing instruments (piano, guitar, flute, violin, drums)

Reading

paperbacks, hardcovers, novels, bestsellers

Places to Visit

museums, galleries, theatre, movies
zoo, aquarium, circus
sports stadium, arena
amusement parks, exhibitions

Discussion Topics

1. What do you like and/or dislike about North American television?

2. What is your favourite and least favourite commercial? Do you think it is effective? Why?

3. Do you think there should be less sex and violence on TV?

4. What books or movies do you enjoy? Why?

5. What kind of music do you enjoy listening to?

6. What are your favourite sports? Do you watch or participate? Do you prefer team or individual sports?

7. If you could start a collection, what would you collect?

8. What genre of art do you like? Do you like modern art?

9. Do you think Canadians have too much or too little leisure time? Do you think they spend their leisure time wisely?

10. What do you find different about leisure time in Canada and in your native country?

Additional Activities

1. Organize some leisure-time activities. Bring some board games and card games to class. In small groups, try to learn new games. Play charades or other party games.

2. Watch a segment of a TV show in class. Analyze it in terms of frequency and quality of commercials, American vs. Canadian content and the presence of violence.

3. Have a classroom debate on one of the following topics:
   (a) Television, movies and books should be more strictly censored.
   (b) Our work week should be reduced and our leisure time increased.
   (c) Television is a negative influence on society.
4. Plan, rehearse and videotape a class production of a news or entertainment show. For example, your class could do a talent show, a documentary on the life of a foreign student, a quiz show or an informative advertisement for your school's ESL programme.

Assignments

1. Prepare a short oral report on your favourite movie, TV show, book or game and present it to the class.
2. Make a list of movies playing in your city and classify them according to type (science fiction, comedy, etc.).
3. Make a summary of the rules of a sport or game.
4. Research one other leisure-time activity that may interest you and describe it to the class.
5. Expand on the list of leisure-time activities given in this unit.

Food For Thought

Dining Out

Because of the multicultural nature of their society, Canadians are exposed to a wide variety of ethnic cuisines. Although ethnic restaurants do not serve the same foods that one could expect in the native country, Canadians expect less "westernization" of ethnic food. For instance, even though milder versions of spicy dishes may be offered, some Canadians have developed a taste for the hot foods found in tropical countries.

Gita:	Let's go out for dinner tonight. We forgot to take something out of the freezer and **it's been ages** since we've been out.
Mike:	Good idea. Where do you feel like going?
Gita:	Oh, **I dunno**. How about the Golden Dragon?
Mike:	We had Chinese food last time. There's a new French place somebody at work was **raving about**.
Gita:	But we're trying to cut back on **cholesterol** and those **rich sauces** are **murder**. Let's look in the Dining Guide in the newspaper.... Hmmm, this Japanese place has good reviews.
Mike:	Nah, that **sushi** we had last time wasn't bad, but...
Gita:	This place is different. The cook cuts up the food and **stir-fries** it at your table. It's supposed to be quite a show.
Mike:	I'm not really in the mood for Oriental cooking tonight. How about steak or roast beef?
Gita:	They're easy enough to cook at home. Seafood?
Mike:	Too expensive. Mexican food?
Gita:	I wish I could, but that spicy food gives me heartburn. Maybe some vegetarian pizza at Angelo's?
Mike:	How about that German place on Main Street? I haven't had good **bratwurst** since the **Oktoberfest** party.
Gita:	No, wait, here's something that sounds interesting — "The Great Canadian **Smorgasbord**" — they claim to have something for everyone.
Mike:	Great, let's go.

it's been ages it's been a long time

I dunno reduced from of "I don't know"

to rave about to speak enthusiastically about

cholesterol thick substance in the blood; high levels may result from eating too much animal fat

rich sauces sauces made with a lot of butter and cream

murder (slang) really bad

sushi small rolls of cold rice with fish and pickled vegetables wrapped in seaweed

stir-fries cooks small pieces of food quickly over high heat with constant stirring; method used in Oriental cooking

bratwurst type of German sausage

Oktoberfest German festival celebrated in October

smorgasbord (or **smorg**) (Swedish word) buffet containing a wide variety of dishes, hot and cold

Discussion

1. How would you characterize Gita's food tastes? And Mike's?
2. What foods do you think will be served at the smorgasbord? What foods would you consider typically Canadian food?
3. Do you like to eat out? What kinds of restaurants do you like?
4. Use a restaurant guide for your city or region and make a list of the types of restaurants.

The Dinner Party

Canadian cooking is sometimes stereotyped as consisting mainly of American-style fast foods — hamburgers, french fries and the like. However, restaurants do not provide a complete picture of what Canadian families eat. Moreover, food in Canada varies according to region, different ethnic influences and individual preferences. Therefore, Canadian food is not as easy to characterize as the food of some other nations.

fast-food restaurants restaurants that offer food such as hamburgers and pizza, served quickly for eat in or take out

cafeteria informal restaurant, especially in schools and office buildings, where customers select food from a counter and take it to the tables themselves

round out complete

starters (informal) first course of a meal, appetizer

veggies (informal) vegetables

a tough one a difficult choice or decision

from scratch from basic ingredients, not prepared as with a mix

saskatoon berries (or **saskatoons**) wild berries that grow from western Ontario to British Columbia and the Yukon; "saskatoon" comes from the Cree word for the fruit (the city was named after the fruit)

do the groceries buy groceries

Barry: I guess we'd better get our menu together for Friday night.

Julia: Oh, that's right. I almost forgot. Your cousin's coming with the two Japanese exchange students.

Barry: Right. And I promised her we'd make a good Canadian meal. After all, they've been eating at the university and in **fast-food restaurants**. This is the first home-cooked meal they're having here.

Julia: I can just imagine what they think of Canadian food if they've been eating at the university **cafeteria**! But what's a typical Canadian meal?

Barry: Good question. I guess a meat-and-potatoes dinner can be considered more typical than something like a pasta dish.

Julia: Roast beef, turkey, salmon?

Barry: How about if I make my breaded, baked chicken?

Julia: Sounds great. And to **round out** the main course, we can have new potatoes, green beans and carrots with dill from our herb garden.

Barry: Do you want a salad for **starters**?

Julia: Maybe raw **veggies** and dip instead. That way we can have the appetizer in the living room and sit and talk for a while.

Barry: Good idea. We can serve pumpkin soup as a first course.

Julia: I can pick up some rolls from the bakery on my way home from work. And dessert?

Barry: That's a **tough one**. We usually have ice cream and fruit, but I think I'd like to bake something **from scratch**.

Julia: Hmmm.... Cheesecake? Blueberry pie? Carrot cake?

Barry: Let's make a couple of fruit pies — offer a choice since it's really no more trouble than making one. How about **saskatoon berries** and strawberry-rhubarb? We still have some of the fruit we picked in the freezer.

Julia: Perfect. Let me make a list of things we'll need to get when we **do the groceries**.

Discussion

1. What do Barry and Julia think of cafeteria food?
2. What do you think of the dinner Barry and Julia are planning? Would you like to eat it?

3. In small groups, make a list of foods you would consider to be typical Canadian food. Then look through Canadian cookbooks and food magazines and make lists of some Canadian dishes.

LANGUAGE NOTES

FOOD IDIOMS

A wide variety of food words and expressions are used in idioms.

Another complaint form? What's he *beefing* about now? (complaining)

She'll have to offer a pretty big *carrot* to get Ivy to take the job. (promised reward, advantage)

He tried to quit smoking *cold turkey*. (suddenly, at once — expression used to describe abrupt method of quitting something to get over an addiction)

I wish she'd learn that you can't *cry over spilt milk* and go on with her life. (regret what has happened)

I didn't go on the trip with them because hiking is just not *my cup of tea*. (the sort of thing I like)

I didn't like the deal he was offering — the whole thing sounded *fishy* to me. (false)

He's got another *half-baked* idea for making money, but I always take what he says *with a grain of salt*. (not sensible, lacking planned judgement; with an unwillingness to accept it)

No trouble at all — it was *a piece of cake*. (easy)

She said she was glad that she didn't get the promotion because she really didn't want to leave Vancouver, but I think it was just *sour grapes*. (the act of pretending to dislike something when it is unobtainable)

I thought I saw some big fish from that lake before, but his catch yesterday *takes the cake*. (is the most outstanding)

EXPRESSIONS WITH "IN" AND "OUT"

There are a number of idiomatic expressions with *in* and *out* in informal English:

I like to *eat out* once in a while — somebody to serve me and no dishes to wash. (eat in a restaurant)

To know how to package the food, the attendant at the fast-food counter asks: "Will that be to *eat in* or *take out*?" (to eat inside the restaurant or to take the food out)

James and Cindy have been *going out* for a long time now. (dating)

Is Mr. Thomas *in*? (in the office)

No, I'm sorry. He just went *out* a few minutes ago. (left)

Fred *knows all the ins and outs* of the insurance business. (is fully experienced in, knows all about)

They say that short skirts will be *in* once again this year and that the baggy look is definitely *out*. (in fashion, in style; out of fashion)

Don't tell me the postal workers are *out* again! (out on strike)

I'd better call you. I'll be *in and out* of the office all day.

Why don't you *go out* for a change and have some fun?

No, I'd better *stay in* and do some work.

CULTURE NOTE

On weekdays, Canadians tend to have a light breakfast — toast, muffins or cereal with juice and coffee. Bacon and eggs, pancakes, french toast and other breakfasts that take more time to prepare are more commonly eaten on the weekend, sometimes later in the day as "brunch."

Lunch is often eaten away from home. While some people eat in restaurants, others "brown-bag," bringing a sandwich from home to eat at work or school. Some people have their main meal, dinner, at midday and have a light supper, but most lunchtime meals consist of soup, a sandwich or a salad.

Canadians usually eat a large meal anywhere from five to nine o'clock in the evening. Some meals may include appetizers, soup or salad before the main course. A typical main course includes meat or fish, potatoes or rice, and one or two vegetables. Dessert is usually served with coffee or tea at the end of the meal.

Canadians often entertain by inviting people to dinner. It is customary to arrive on time for a dinner party and to bring a bottle of wine or a small impersonal gift, such as flowers or candy. Food is not brought unless specifically asked for by the hosts, as, for example, at a potluck dinner, where everyone contributes a food item.

Table manners can vary from culture to culture. Even the way utensils are handled can be different. In Europe, diners tend to keep their forks in the left hand throughout a meal; in North America the fork is often switched to the right hand after food is cut. Sometimes a dinner is served as a buffet; people then serve themselves from a table that is set with a variety of foods.

Some families will say grace (a prayer of thanks) before a meal. It is polite to finish all the food on a plate, if possible. An empty or near empty wine glass will be continually refilled by the hosts. Canadians consider it impolite to make noise while eating. To show that you enjoyed a meal, it is polite to compliment the quality of the food. Be sure to accept a second helping if you like the food and are not full; Canadian hosts will usually offer it only once and will take a refusal at face value. In some other cultures, however, it is polite to refuse for up to three times before accepting a second helping.

Food likes and dislikes vary greatly from culture to culture and can be a source of intense personal prejudice. What is disgusting to one person can be a delicacy to another. In addition to personal preference, people may have dietary restrictions because of religion or for health reasons, such as allergies. Hosts may inquire about such restrictions or offer a variety of foods when they do not know their guests well.

FOOD GAMES

Some of the games that follow are based on a number of traditional word games, but they use food names instead of other words. The games should be prepared ahead of time.

THE MOST IMPORTANT FOOD IN THE WORLD

Write the names of different foods on slips of paper. Each student draws the name of a food item and has two minutes to argue that this food is the most important food in the world, and that society could not function without it. For example:

"We could not exist without pumpkin. It can be eaten as a vegetable and made into baked goods such as pie and bread. Thanksgiving and Halloween depend on the pumpkin. How scary would a jack o'lantern be if it were carved from a potato? The size and colour of the pumpkin make it valuable for decoration. And besides, how would Cinderella have got to the ball without the pumpkin?"

You can make teams and award points for the best arguments.

TWENTY QUESTIONS

Write the names of different foods on slips of paper. In teams, draw slips. Try to guess the name of the opposing team's food using only yes-or-no questions. The questions should move from general to more specific. For example, the first questions may establish the category of the food, such as "Is it a fruit?" Team members can take turns asking questions of the opposing team. Try to guess the food in less than 20 questions.

PASSWORD

Once again, draw slips of paper on which names of foods have been written. Work in pairs to try to get your partner to guess the name of the food you have drawn. Describe the food without saying its name. For example:

"It's a vegetable that is long and green. It looks like a cucumber but belongs to the squash family. It is often cooked with Italian dishes." (zucchini)

Have a time limit for guessing and switch roles so that you both have turns describing and guessing.

DISH DICTIONARY

Dictionary is a game in which one player chooses a word from the dictionary and reads the word to the group. The player choosing the word writes the correct definition on a slip of paper while everyone else writes a possible definition on a slip of paper. The definitions are mixed together. Each player draws a definition and reads it aloud. The players try to guess which one is correct.

In this version, use the names of dishes chosen from cookbooks and have players guess the main ingredients. Try to use a variety of ethnic dishes and pick unusual and interesting dishes. (For example, one version of spice cake made in North America has a can of tomato soup as a main ingredient.)

Play this game in small groups. Have one person read aloud the name of the dish and have each player write down a brief description on a slip of paper. The person who has chosen the dish writes down the correct definition. Mix up the definitions and read them aloud. Guess which one is correct.

RECIPE JIGSAW

Bring a copy of a simple recipe to class. The teacher chooses three or four recipes and writes or types them out so that each step of the instructions is on a separate line. Cut out each step of all the recipes and mix them up. Each student gets one piece of a recipe and has to find the students with the rest of that recipe. See how fast you can reassemble the recipes.

Additional Vocabulary

brunch   a combination of breakfast and lunch, served late in the morning or early afternoon, usually on Sunday

drive-through   take-out system; you order through an intercom, pick up your food at the window and take it home without leaving your car

licensed restaurant   place that has a liquor licence to serve beer, wine and other alcoholic beverages

caterer   person who handles the food preparation for parties and banquets, usually served in a home or rented premises

barbecue   several uses are common: outdoor grill; meat cooked on a grill; spicy tomato sauce used on the food; party or picnic where barbecued foods are served

cuisine   (Fr.) style of cooking

gourmet   (Fr.) someone who enjoys and is an excellent judge of high quality food and drink.

Discussion Topics

1. Describe some Canadian eating customs that are different from those in your native culture.
2. Describe your favourite meal.
3. Do you like to shop for food? What do you think of food prices and availability in Canada? How do you shop for bargains?

Additional Activities

1. Look at a few sample menus and discuss the foods available and their prices. Practise placing orders from the menus.
2. In small groups, look at different cookbooks to see how recipes are written. Discuss the different foods. Try out a simple recipe in class.
3. Have a potluck supper including various ethnic foods.

Assignments

1. Make a list of the different kinds of ethnic restaurants in your city or region.
2. Make a shopping list for a special meal and consult the food store ads in the newspaper to find the best prices for the foods on your list.
3. Locate an interesting recipe in the food section of your newspaper. Identify common cooking terms.
4. Read the restaurant reviews in a newspaper or magazine. Prepare your own review of a restaurant you have tried and present it to the class.

Survival of the Fittest

The Fitness Craze

Canadians enjoy a variety of activities that help them to stay fit. Swimming, walking, biking and lifting weights are popular activities. Exercise classes are conducted at community centres, sports clubs and school gymnasiums. The government also encourages the fitness craze with its "Participaction" programme.

bushed (slang) tired, exhausted

work-out intense exercise session

aerobics exercises designed to increase heart action

have two left feet (idiomatic) be clumsy, unable to dance

Fred Astaire well-known American dancer

self-conscious uncomfortably aware of one's own appearance, embarrassed

huffing and puffing (colloquial) breathing hard

epidemic a widespread occurrence of something; usually used for diseases

baby boomers the large number of people born during the baby boom (1946–1962)

Y short for Y.M.C.A. (Young Men's Christian Association) or Y.W.C.A. (Young Women's Christian Association), organizations that run various social and community programmes

jump on the bandwagon (idiomatic) join in on what everyone else is doing

no sweat (slang) no problem

Janice:	So when are we going to get together to finish off this report?
Debbie:	Well, I'm free most of the week. Tuesdays and Thursdays I have my fitness class, though.
Janice:	Fitness class! How do you find the energy? After a day in here, I'm too **bushed** for anything but supper and TV.
Debbie:	But I find that getting a good **work-out** a couple times a week actually makes me feel more energetic. You should try it.
Janice:	What kind of class is it?
Debbie:	**Aerobics** — it's fun, a lot of dance-type steps.
Janice:	Dance? **I've got two left feet** — I can't dance.
Stuart:	(joining the conversation) Don't worry about it, Jan. I'm no **Fred Astaire** myself. When I first started aerobics I felt pretty **self-conscious**, but everybody's too busy **huffing and puffing** to notice anyone else.
Janice:	You take aerobics, too! What is this — an **epidemic**?
Debbie:	Sure, haven't you heard? Fitness is a big thing with us aging **baby boomers**. Why don't you come and try out my class? They have a drop-in fee if you're not a regular.
Janice:	I don't know about this. Where is this class anyway?
Debbie:	It's at the community centre near my place.
Janice:	Is that where you go too, Stu?
Stuart:	No, the **Y** down the street — I go on my lunch hour.
Janice:	I suppose I might as well **jump on the bandwagon**, as they say. But it'll probably kill me.
Stuart:	**No sweat.** Just take it easy the first night.

Discussion

1. Where could this conversation be taking place?

2. Can you find the pun (play on words) in this dialogue?

3. What is your favourite way to keep fit? Why do you enjoy it?

4. Change the dialogue so that Debbie is trying to persuade Janice to go jogging or swimming. Practise dialogue variations in pairs.

5. Some companies now offer fitness breaks instead of coffee breaks and have gym facilities at the workplace. What do you think of this trend? Can you think of similar ways to make fitness activities more accessible?

Health Food!?

A glance through food magazines and cookbooks shows that the types of food Canadians eat has changed a lot over the last few decades. Food follows fashions and fads just as much as clothing does. More exotic fruits and vegetables are available today and different ethnic cuisines have influenced Canadian tastes. However, probably the biggest change is due to the link between health and eating habits. Generally, Canadians have cut down on fat, red meat, salt and sugar.

Liz:	Supper's ready, **hon**.
Gary:	Okay, I'm coming.... Hey, what's this? A salad for supper?
Liz:	Well, it's too hot to cook. And anyway, it's good for you. The doctor said you should eat more greens.
Gary:	How do you expect me to survive on **rabbit food**?
Liz:	**C'mon**, it's not so bad. There's tuna in there for protein, as well as the lettuce and vegetables.
Gary:	All right, all right.... Where's the white bread?
Liz:	I didn't buy any. Here's some whole wheat rolls — more **fibre**, you know.
Gary:	Did you **do away with** dessert, too?
Liz:	Well, I know what a **sweet tooth** you have, so I made a fruit dessert. You'll never know it's **low-cal**.
Gary:	Last year you **nagged me into** quitting smoking and now you're trying to reform my eating habits — when will it all end?
Liz:	When you're perfect. Besides, I only do it because I care about you.... Oh, and **easy on the salt**.

hon   short for "honey," a term of endearment

rabbit food   (slang, derogatory) salad, green vegetables

c'mon   reduced form of "come on," interjection meaning "You must be kidding"

fibre   stringy part of plant material that aids digestion

do away with   (colloquial) get rid of, abolish, destroy, kill

to have a sweet tooth   (idiomatic) to be fond of sweets and desserts

low-cal   low in calories, non-fattening

nag into   continually complain and remind until a habit is changed

easy on the salt   use the salt sparingly or lightly

Discussion

1. Where do you think this dialogue is taking place? What is the relationship between Liz and Gary?

2. Describe how Liz is trying to improve Gary's health. What do you think of the health food craze?

3. In small groups, make a list of foods that are considered healthy and those that are not. Decide on five tips for eating well. Compare your list with those of other groups and discuss any differences.

Visiting Hours

Hospital rules concerning visitors vary according to the ward (the section of the hospital) and the situation. It's a good idea to check ahead to see if the patient is well enough to receive visitors.

stir crazy   (slang) mentally unbalanced due to being locked up

traction   state of having leg or arm pulled by a device to relieve pressure or pull a broken bone into position

hobbling   walk with difficulty, in an awkward way

a bad break   bad luck

pun   play on words, joke where a word can mean two different things

unintentional   not done on purpose

soaps (soap operas)   dramatic television shows, usually shown in the afternoon, which tell of personal relationships between the characters in serial format; the name results from the fact that these dramas were often sponsored by soap companies

Yuri: Hi Alice. How are you doing?

Alice: Yuri! And Trish! Hey, it's good to see you guys!

Trish: Goin' **stir crazy** already, huh?

Alice: Let's just say that lying flat on my back with my leg in **traction** is not the way I wanted to spend my holiday.

Yuri: So when will you be getting out of this place?

Alice: Pretty soon now, I think. They still have to put the cast on. But I'll be **hobbling** around on crutches for weeks.

Trish: What **a bad break** for you. Oops, sorry. The **pun** was unintentional.

Yuri: Ignore Trish's bad jokes and tell me more about this ski accident.

Alice: Well, I was skiing down the Bowl at Lake Louise. I hit an icy patch and I just plain slipped. My bindings did not release and my skis got tangled up as I slid.

Trish: I can't believe it. You're such a good skier.

Alice: You know how it goes. Anyone can have an accident.

Yuri: Hans said you had quite the ride down the mountain.

Alice: Yeah. The ski patrol took me down in a sled. It was wild! They strapped me in so I couldn't move at all.

Trish: Sounds like quite the tale you'll be able to tell around the ski lodge.

Yuri: Oh, I almost forgot. We brought you some stuff. We made you some chocolate chip cookies.

Trish: And I brought you some magazines and a couple paperbacks.

Alice: Great. This stuff'll be better than watching the **soaps** all afternoon. Thanks a lot, guys.

Discussion

1. In your own words, explain why Alice is in the hospital.

2. What did Yuri and Trish bring for Alice? Do you think these are appropriate gifts? What else could they have brought? In groups, make a short list of appropriate gifts to bring someone in the hospital.

3. Discuss your experiences as a patient or a visitor in hospital.

4. Discuss guidelines for visiting patients in the hospital or at home. How long should a visit last? How should someone check to make sure the patient is up to receiving visitors? What are suitable topics of conversation?

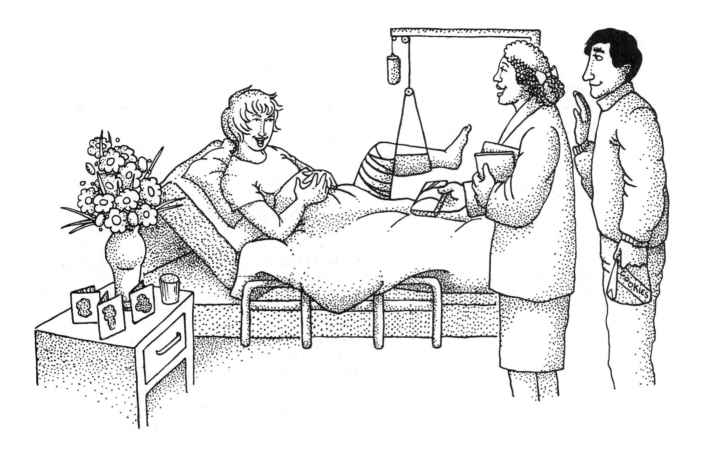

LANGUAGE NOTES

NICKNAMES AND TERMS OF ADDRESS

Many names in English have shortened forms that are used as nicknames. Some people do not like nicknames, however, and others may prefer one particular nickname over others. It is best to find out about personal preferences before using a nickname.

Examples of Nicknames

Alexander — Al, Alex, Sandy
Barbara — Barb, Barbie, Babs
Charles — Charlie, Chuck
Edward — Ed, Eddie, Ted, Ned
Elizabeth — Liz, Eliza, Beth, Bess, Lizzie, Elly, Betty
Katherine — Kathy, Kate, Kit, Kitty, Katie, Kay
Margaret — Marge, Meg, Margie, Peggy, Margo, Greta, Rita

Michael — Mike, Mick, Micky
Patricia — Pat, Patty, Tricia, Trish
Robert — Bob, Rob, Bobby, Robbie
Teresa — Tess, Terry, Tessa, Tracy
William — Will, Bill, Willie, Billy

Nicknames ending in -y or -ie are often used for children.

Some nicknames are not shortened forms of given names. For example, "Chip" is sometimes used as a nickname for a boy who has the same name as his father with the addition of "Junior." Other nicknames are based on physical characteristics or personality traits. A red-haired person may sometimes be called "Red" and a tall person may have the nickname "Stretch." However, these nicknames seem less common today.

Special forms of endearment may be used between a husband and wife or a boyfriend and girlfriend. In English, common endearments include "honey," "sweetheart," "darling," "sugar," "dear."

Other forms of address, often used in order to get someone's attention, include "buddy," "mac," "hey you," "dearie." These terms, however, are very informal and may be considered offensive. Although you may hear them, they should be avoided.

A helpful rule to remember is that the form of the name given in an introduction usually reflects an individual's preference.

GIVING ADVICE

Giving advice is always difficult to do tactfully. Many people resent getting advice and, even when they ask for it, they may be simply seeking approval for what they want to do.

The modal or auxiliary verbs *should* and *ought to* are commonly used to give advice; however, they are quite strong when used without qualifying phrases:

> You should quit smoking.
> You ought to get that transmission checked.

An opening phrase and a tentative tone of voice can make such suggestions more polite:

> I think you should...
> It seems to me that you could...

Modal verbs such as *might* and *may* can further soften a suggestion:

> Joining an exercise class might be a good idea.

Using a rising intonation makes a suggestion more like a question:

> Perhaps you might want to look for a new job?

Clarifying the pros and cons of a problem is also a tactful way of giving advice:

> One advantage of a holiday is that you'll have time to relax; however, it might be too costly right now.

On the other hand, to make a suggestion more forceful, the speaker may begin with a phrase that indicates conviction:

> I believe this would be the better road to take.

The most forceful way to state an opinion or give advice is to state it bluntly without qualifiers:

> This is a serious problem and you must do something about it immediately.

The tone of voice accompanying any suggestion or advice is very important. For instance, tentative suggestions require an encouraging and mild tone. On the other hand, a strong opinion or conviction requires a more forceful and firmer tone.

Provide an appropriate modal auxiliary for the following sentences according to the kind of advice that is being offered.

1. You really _____ get your hair cut! It looks so long and shaggy.
2. I thought that you _____ want to consider several different kinds of diets before choosing one.
3. His hacking and coughing are really getting out of hand; he _____ quit smoking!
4. If you don't want to eat Italian food tonight, you _____ prefer going out to an ordinary restaurant.
5. On the one hand, you have quite a bit of money saved; on the other hand, you _____ want to blow it all on a spa membership!

PUNS

Non-native speakers of a language often have difficulty understanding jokes made in that language. Not only do the concepts of humour vary from one culture to a next, but a lot of humour, such as riddles and jokes, is verbal.

A pun, also called a play on words, is a type of joke that depends on the different meanings of words or sound-alike words. For example, in the first dialogue "no sweat" is used to mean "with no difficulty," but, of course, in an exercise class there is a lot of sweat, or perspiration. In the third dialogue, "break" is used to refer to luck, but it can also refer to a break in a bone.

CULTURE NOTE

Canadians have had government health insurance since the 1960s. The health care system is partly funded by the federal government, but it is administered by the provinces. Therefore, the system is different in each province.

A government-sponsored health care system protects people from having thousands of dollars of debts because of illness. It is generally agreed that Canadians enjoy a high quality of health care, but the system is not without problems. Health care issues focus on medical ethics and the economics and quality of health care.

Two of the more controversial issues surrounding medical ethics are euthanasia (mercy killing) and abortion. Decisions about such procedures are not simply made by the doctor and the patient; government laws and regulations and hospital policy are involved.

High technology has changed the practice of medicine drastically. For example, life support systems have made it possible to keep patients alive beyond the time they would naturally survive. But is this always the right thing to do?

High technology also adds to the costs of health care. Provincial governments spend about a third of their budgets on health care. Some cost-cutting methods have, surprisingly, proved beneficial to patients. For instance, since the home is a much more comfortable environment than a hospital, some patients recover more quickly if they have a shorter hospital stay and are visited at home by a nurse.

Another trend in Canadian medicine is using a team of health care professionals rather than relying solely on the doctor. For example, community health centres provide an alternative to clinics or doctors' offices. And some provinces are developing policies concerning the use of midwives for routine births, with doctors called in when necessary.

While research in drug therapy and advances in medical equipment continue, not all of medicine is high science. Some people who are dissatisfied with modern medicine seek out herbalists and holistic healers. Psychology is also an important part of medicine, as the patient's state of mind is recognized as important in the healing process.

Treatment is not the only aspect of medicine. A healthier lifestyle leads to fewer medical problems. Heart disease and cancer are only two of the major diseases that have been linked to diet, smoking and lack of exercise. Canadians believe in the proverb that says "An ounce of prevention is worth a pound of cure."

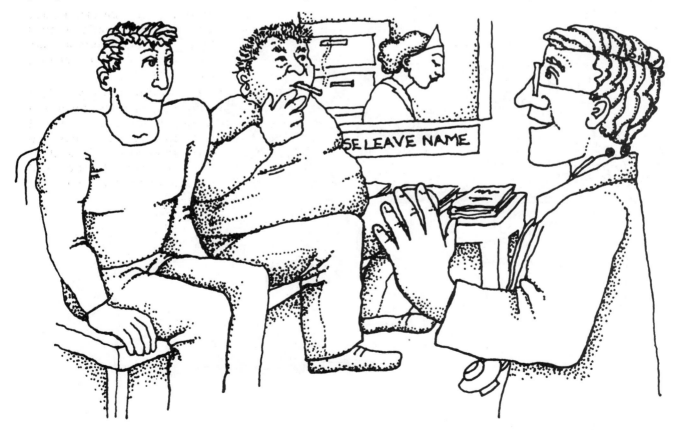

HEALTH AND FITNESS QUIZ

Questionnaires or quizzes are popular items in magazines and newspapers. They are often used to shed light on behaviour and personality, but they are not to be taken too seriously. They are usually in a multiple-choice or true-or-false format.

People who work too hard, workaholics, are prone to heart attacks and other health problems. A balanced lifestyle with time to relax is important for good health. The following quiz tests whether you are a workaholic or not. In small groups, read the questions and choices to each other. Keep a record of your choices and score yourself to find out which category you fall into. Discuss the results with your group. Do you think the test is accurate?

ARE YOU A WORKAHOLIC?

1. What is the first thing you think of when your alarm goes off in the morning?
   a) Oh, boy, time to go to work!
   b) Stupid alarm.
   c) I wonder what the news/weather/traffic report says.
   d) Where's my coffee?
   e) What excuse can I find for not going to work?

2. It's Friday afternoon. What are you thinking about?
   a) working hard on the last bit of work so you can clear your desk before you leave
   b) leaving home early to beat the traffic and taking off for the weekend
   c) which work to take home with you on the weekend
   d) putting in a couple extra hours of work and leaving late
   e) what fun will you have on the weekend

3. Which section of the newspaper is your favourite?
   a) news
   b) sports
   c) business
   d) entertainment
   e) comics

4. You have two weeks' holiday. What do you intend to do?
   a) go to a resort and forget everything about work
   b) spend some of your vacation time on work-related business
   c) not take your holidays because you want to work
   d) take a trip filled with educational activities such as trips to museums
   e) go on a trip with some friends from work

5. The best reason to have a home computer is:
   a) to play educational games
   b) to set up telecommuting, working at home rather than in the office
   c) to bring home work to do in the evening and weekends
   d) to hook up with various information services
   e) to play mindless arcade games

6. If your house is on fire, what will you grab as you go out the door?
   a) your briefcase
   b) your wallet or purse
   c) your jewelry box
   d) your favourite teddy bear
   e) your photograph album

7. What are your favourite clothes?
   a) bathing suit
   b) blue jeans
   c) business suit
   d) party clothes
   e) work overalls

8. You're leaving work to meet a friend who's visiting from out of town, but your boss asks you to stay later to finish some work. How will you react?
   a) refuse to stay because of your plans
   b) agree to stay without hesitation
   c) call your friend to say you will be late and try to get out early
   d) ask your friend to meet you at work
   e) explain about the meeting and ask if you can arrange to do the work at another time

9. You've got a business trip in Quebec City and your spouse wants to come along. What do you do?
   a) make up an excuse so you can go alone to concentrate on work
   b) bring your spouse and try to combine business and pleasure
   c) bring your spouse but make it clear he or she sightsees alone while you work
   d) bring your spouse, concentrate on your work for a few days and stay longer for a vacation
   e) promise your spouse that you will go on a trip to Quebec City another time

10. Where would you like to be in ten years?
    a) the president of your company or organization
    b) a lottery winner and retired
    c) richer and more successful
    d) still working but with a family and a nice house and time to enjoy them
    e) it doesn't matter what position you have as long as you enjoy the work

Answer Key

Score your answers as shown below. Then add up the scores to find out which label best applies to you.

1)	a–5	b–2	c–4	d–3	e–1
2)	a–3	b–1	c–5	d–4	e–2
3)	a–4	b–2	c–5	d–2	e–1
4)	a–1	b–4	c–5	d–2	e–3
5)	a–2	b–3	c–5	d–4	e–1
6)	a–5	b–4	c–3	d–1	e–2
7)	a–1	b–2	c–5	d–2	e–4
8)	a–1	b–5	c–3	d–4	e–2
9)	a–5	b–1	c–4	d–2	e–3
10)	a–5	b–1	c–4	d–2	e–3

44-50 — **Superworkaholic.** Your work is your passion. There's no hope for you.

35-43 — **Workaholic.** Your work is your reason for living. You need to find other interests.

25-34 — **Well-balanced person.** Your work is important but not the only thing in your life. You know how to handle your life.

17-24 — **Underachiever.** You do your work because you have to. Maybe you should find a job you enjoy more.

10-16 — **Party animal.** For you, work is a four-letter word and fun is the most important thing.

WRITE YOUR OWN HEALTH AND FITNESS QUIZ

Divide the class into groups of three to five students. Write a short questionnaire (up to ten questions) for a physical or mental health topic. Use the workaholic one as a guide. The questionnaire can be serious or slightly humorous.

Suggestions for topics are:

How healthy is your lifestyle?
Are you a fitness nut?
Are you a chocoholic?   (addicted to chocolate)
Are you a couch potato?   (someone who dislikes physical activity)

Are you a health food nut?
Are you a neatnik?   (obsessed with making everything neat and tidy)
Are you a hypochondriac?
Are you superstitious?
Are you addicted to _____ ?   (e.g., cigarettes, beer, TV)
Do you have a sweet tooth?
Are you health conscious?
Are you a compulsive eater?

Additional Vocabulary

G.P.   general practitioner, physician who provides general health care

specialist   physician who specializes in one area of medicine (e.g., plastic surgery, obstetrics, neurology)

clinic   facility where a group of doctors work together outside the hospital

hypochondriac   a person who imagines he or she has an illness

prescription drugs   drugs that are ordered by the doctor, as opposed to over-the-counter medication bought in a drugstore without a prescription (e.g., aspirin)

out-patient care   treatment in a hospital that does not require an overnight stay

jock   (slang) person who participates in many sports

Discussion Topics

1. What are the advantages and disadvantages of Canada's health care system?

2. What is the best way to stay healthy and live a long life?

3. Do you believe in folk and herbal remedies? What kinds? Do you have any home remedies for a cold or other common ailment?

4. What is your opinion of your city's smoking by-laws? Are they effective? Should people be allowed to smoke wherever they wish?

Additional Activities

1. Hold a class debate on one of the following topics:
   a) Patients and their families should be able to make more decisions about their care, including the use of life support systems.
   b) Doctors should be able to charge their patients additional fees rather than being restricted to the amounts from government health plans.
   c) For health care issues, public good is more important than individual rights. (Consider specific issues such as vaccination, smoking and the use of protective devices such as seat belts and bicycle helmets.)

2. In small groups, make vocabulary lists of some common medical terms.

3. In pairs, practise various dialogues:
   a) a doctor-patient discussion on improving the patient's general health;
   b) a reporter interviewing a famous athlete on his or her training program;
   c) a prospective medical student being interviewed on why he or she wishes to become a doctor.

Assignments

1. Research the history of medicare in Canada.

2. Make a list of different kinds of specialists. (Some are listed in the Yellow Pages under "Physicians.")

3. Find out about a recreation/sports facility near you and report to the class on the activities offered.

It's Customary

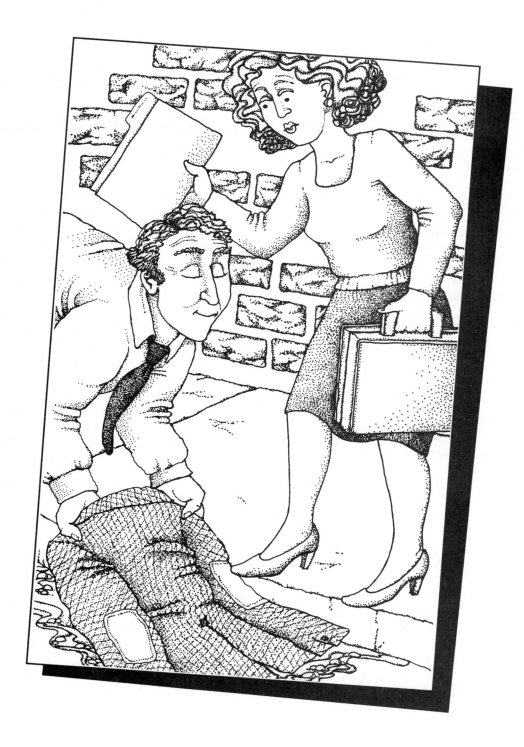

7

A Letter to the Advice Column

Many customs are based on etiquette, the formal rules for proper behaviour in society. Good manners are important in both business and social situations. However, because of today's hectic lifestyles, less emphasis seems to be placed on good manners; for example, children do not learn formal manners for meals if their families do not have formal dinners. Moreover, as society changes, the rules for polite behaviour change, and it is difficult to keep up-to-date.

at my mother's knee (idiomatic) from my mother

at a loss confused, unsure of what to do

courtesies polite or thoughtful acts or expressions

pointers useful hints or suggestions

chauvinist man who thinks women are inferior; (original meaning) an overly patriotic person

rule of thumb (idiomatic) practical rule that has proven useful through experience

yo-yo a child's toy that bobs up and down

Dear Ms. Mannerly,

I learned the rules for the proper way to treat a lady **at my mother's knee** many years ago. But these rules do not seem to hold in these days of equal treatment for women, and I'm **at a loss** when it comes to the everyday **courtesies** I used to extend to them. Is it still correct to open doors and to give up your seat on the bus to women? What about standing up when they enter the room? I need some **pointers**.

Trying not to be a **chauvinist**

Dear Trying,

Common courtesy and practicality are good **rules of thumb**. You should always offer your seat on the bus to pregnant women, elderly people and anyone who may have trouble standing. There is no need to offer seats to young, healthy women, just as it is no longer necessary to go out of your way to open doors for them. Open a door for anyone who might have trouble with it — anyone carrying packages or books, for example — and hold a door for someone coming after you. Standing up each time a woman enters the room can make you feel like a **yo-yo** and is no longer necessary in these days of informal comings and goings. Standing up for an introduction, however, is polite. Don't throw out all those rules that your mother taught you, just use common sense to adjust them to the circumstances.

M. J. Mannerly

Discussion

1. In your own words, briefly explain the problem in this letter and the advice given in the reply.
2. Role play a talk show with classmates. Appoint a team of etiquette experts. Classmates ask the experts various questions, for example:

   At a very formal dinner, which fork should be used first?

   If a couple breaks up, should both people be invited to parties by their friends?

   Is it polite to eat chicken with your fingers?

   Use etiquette books and newspaper advice columns if you need some help.

3. Discuss the importance of good manners in today's society.

A Housewarming

Social engagements involve a number of customs. The invitation determines the type of activity and therefore the type of customs to be followed. A housewarming party traditionally calls for a small gift of a household item for the hosts, but today housewarmings are often considered to be just parties and not gift-giving occasions.

Vicky: Hey, **wait up you guys**! I've been looking all over for you.

Karuma: Oh, hi Vicky. **What's up**?

Vicky: Well, Gaston and I are **having some people over** Saturday night — sort of a **housewarming** party for the new place now that all the drywall and paint have been put away **for good**. Anyway, I was wondering if you two would like to come.

Stan: Oh, that sounds great. What time?

Vicky: Um, **eightish**.

Stan: Can I bring anything?

Vicky: Well, it's basically **a wine 'n cheese** and if you want to bring a bottle — that would be fine. Oh, and dress casually — it won't be anything fancy.

Karuma: Well, I'm afraid I won't be able to make it. I'm going out of town for the weekend.

Vicky: That's too bad. I wanted to show you what we've done with the place. You haven't seen it since before the big renovations started.

Karuma: I guess I'll have to take a **raincheck** on that. Can I get the grand tour some other time?

Vicky: Sure. Why don't you drop by sometime?

Karuma: I'll give you a call when I come back. Maybe we can set something up.

Vicky: Oh, and Stan — you do have my address, don't you?

Stan: No, **come to think of it**, I don't. **Hang on** while I get a pen.

wait up (colloquial) wait for me

you guys (slang) term of address, used for both males and females

what's up what's new, what's the matter

to have someone over to have visitors

housewarming party celebrating a move into a new home

for good (colloquial) forever, permanently

eightish (colloquial) around eight

a wine 'n cheese party where wine and cheese are the main refreshments ("party" has been dropped off the end of the phrase)

rain check understanding that an offer will be renewed at another time

come to think of it (colloquial) as I think of it, actually

hang on — (colloquial) wait

Discussion

1. Is this a formal or an informal invitation?

2. Imagine you are the guests at Vicky and Gaston's housewarming party. In small groups, talk over your plans (what to bring, what to wear, how to get there, etc.).

3. Modify the dialogue by changing the type of party and Karuma's excuse. Role play the dialogue for the class.

4. Discuss customs involved in visiting someone for dinner, a party or an overnight stay. Compare Canadian customs with those in your native country.

Canadian Holidays

Many customs surround holiday celebrations. The list below describes some of the most common holidays celebrated in Canada. Legal holidays are marked with an asterisk (*). Other holidays and celebrations may be regional (Quebec has a holiday on June 24, while some provinces have a holiday on the first Monday in August) or ethnic (such as St. Patrick's Day, March 17). Some Christian holidays, such as Easter and Christmas, have become so well-established in Canada that they also have non-religious significance and are celebrated by non-Christians.

St. Valentine's Day (*February 14th*) is a day to send romantic, sentimental gifts (especially flowers and jewelry) to a spouse or sweetheart. Children often exchange valentine cards with friends. The phrase "Be my valentine" means "Be my love." The day is symbolized by hearts, flowers, red and pink cards and Cupid, an angelic child with a bow and arrow.

Easter * is usually in March or April, but the date varies. A four-day long weekend, including Good Friday and Easter Monday, is often given as a holiday from work or school. While primarily a religious holiday commemorating the resurrection of Christ, Easter also means the arrival of spring. Children hunt for Easter eggs hidden by the Easter bunny in and around their home. They colour eggs and are often given gifts of chocolate. Easter supper is traditionally ham, lamb or turkey. Symbols of Easter include eggs, baby animals (rabbits, chicks, lambs), Easter hats, baskets filled with goodies and the Easter lily.

Mother's Day (*second Sunday in May*) is a day to treat Mother (breakfast in bed or dinner out) and give her gifts and flowers.

Father's Day (*third Sunday in June*) is a day to treat Father and give him gifts.

Victoria Day * (*the Monday on or before May 24th*) commemorates Queen Victoria's birthday. This long weekend marks the beginning of the summer season for most tourist sites; the season usually ends with the Thanksgiving weekend. Picnics and fireworks are part of the traditional celebrations.

Canada Day * (*July 1st*) marks the day Canada officially became a country (in 1867) — in other words, Canada's birthday. It is celebrated with parades, community picnics, fireworks and other festivities. The prominent symbol is, of course, the national flag.

Labour Day * (*first Monday in September*) is a holiday in honour of the work force, but it is generally just celebrated as the last day of summer holidays, the last day before school starts again.

Thanksgiving * (*second Monday in October*) celebrates the harvest. The traditional meal includes turkey with cranberry sauce, fall vegetables (squash, potatoes) and pumpkin pie. Symbols include harvest vegetables (especially in a cornucopia — a horn of plenty), turkeys and the colourful fall leaves.

=(All Hallows Eve)= Hallowe'en = Hallowe evening   希望读 "Waterford."

Halloween (*October 31st*) is the eve of All Saints' Day when ghosts, goblins, witches and other supernatural phenomena are supposed to be out haunting. Children often go door-to-door dressed in costumes, shouting "Trick or Treat," and by the end of the evening they have bags full of treats (candies). (The treats are traditionally bribes to keep away the spirits, symbolized by the children.) Adults often have costume parties. Symbols include witches, ghosts, jack-o'-lanterns (carved pumpkins with faces) and monsters.

=南瓜灯.

observed (l1:11:11)

Remembrance Day * (*November 11th*) commemorates the end of World War I and honours the soldiers who died in the wars. War memorials are visited, wreaths are laid at graves and a minute's silence is <u>observed</u> at 11 a.m. People wear poppies, red flowers with a black centre. It is a day off work and school in some parts of Canada.

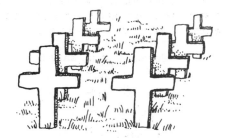

Christmas Day * (*December 25th*) is the most celebrated holiday of the year — celebrations go on for weeks. Christmas is a time for partying, visiting family and friends, sending cards and giving gifts. Festivities vary according to ethnic and individual family traditions. Traditional foods include turkey, fruit cake, cookies, candies, plum pudding and many other specialties. There are countless famous songs and stories for Christmas time. Symbols include the Nativity scene commemorating Christ's birth, Santa Claus and his reindeer, stockings filled with gifts, brightly coloured packages, snowmen and the Christmas tree with its traditional decorations (bells, stars, angels, candy canes, lights, etc.).

New Year's Eve (*December 31st*) is a night for partying to "ring out the old year and ring in the new." At midnight people cheer, kiss, toast each other and sing "Auld Lang Syne." An old man and a young baby symbolize the old and the new year, respectively.

New Year's Day * (*January 1st*) is usually a time of family get-togethers. It is considered part of the Christmas time celebrations.

Discussion

1. Describe other Canadian regional and ethnic holidays that you are familiar with.
2. In small groups, plan a celebration for the next holiday on the calendar. Research the origins of the customs for that holiday.
3. Compare your native country's celebrations to the holidays in Canada.

LANGUAGE NOTES

INVITATIONS

Generally, the more formal the occasion, the more formal the invitation. Invitations to weddings and formal parties are usually written or printed on special cards. "R.S.V.P." ("répondez s'il vous plait," French for "please reply") is often written on an invitation and means that the host wishes to know if you are coming or not. Wedding invitations may have formal R.S.V.P. cards to return, while less formal invitations, such as those to a birthday party, may include a phone number to call.

A formal invitation may be worded as follows:

James Hobson, Mary Hobson-Burke,

and Lynn Hobson

request the honour of your presence

at the 50th wedding anniversary celebration

for their parents

Robert and Gillian Hobson

on Saturday, July 15, 1986, at 6 p.m.

Glenview Community Hall,
598 Barview Place,
North Bay, Ontario   R.S.V.P.

Compare these examples of informal invitations:

Would you like to come to dinner on Sunday?
Do you want to come over to my place after work?
How about going for a coffee?
Are you doing anything this weekend? We're having a small get-together Saturday night...
Hey, if you're not busy, um, I thought we could go out for a pizza tonight...

The following expressions may be used to accept an informal invitation:

Thanks, I'd love to.
Okay, sounds good.
That'd be great.
Great, I'll be there.

It is considered polite to give a reason for declining an invitation:

Oh, I'm sorry. I have to visit my brother and his family tomorrow.

Sorry, I can't make it today. How about next week?
Thanks for asking but I've made other plans for Saturday.

Many invitations are indefinite:

We should get together sometime for lunch.
Why don't we go over there sometime and check it out?
Drop by sometime.

These invitations are quite casual and are usually followed by a more definite invitation later.

OFFERS AND REQUESTS

Modal verbs such as *can, could* and *would* are often used to make polite requests and offers. Discuss the degree of formality in the following examples.

Offers and Invitations

Can I bring something?
I could do that for you, if you're having trouble.
Can I get you something else? Another cup of coffee, perhaps?
Would you like to go out tonight?
Would you like some more coffee?

Requests and Orders

Can you open the door for me, please?
You can let me off here, thanks.
Could you move your chair a little?
Would you hand me that book?
Would you wait a few more minutes, please?
I would like to look at some sofa-beds.
I would rather watch a movie than a hockey game.

Make the following interrogatives and imperatives into polite offers and requests:

1. Lend me a pencil.
2. Show me some microwave ovens. (in a store)
3. Want some cake?
4. Move out of the way.
5. Want to see a movie tonight?

CULTURE NOTE

Many customs and traditions found in a culture are based on superstition. Superstitions often have interesting explanations, many of which are based on religious beliefs. For example, black cats are unlucky because they were thought to be symbols of the Devil. Often the original reason behind the belief has been long forgotten, but the superstition persists.

Generally, Canadians are not considered to be very superstitious, but traditions thought to bring luck can dominate certain situations. Wedding customs, for example, involve many superstitions about bringing the couple good luck.

Some people have their own "lucky" numbers, but some numbers are generally thought to be significant. The number 13 is considered unlucky in Canadian culture, for example. Friday 13 is an unlucky day, and many high-rises do not have a thirteenth floor. On the other hand, the numbers 3 and 7 are considered lucky.

Traditional luck charms include a rabbit's foot, a four-leaf clover, a penny and a horseshoe. Some people have their own charms or traditions to bring them luck. For example, they may use a "lucky" pen to write an exam or fill out a lottery ticket. Some people have rituals in their everyday lives, such as following certain routes or doing things in a special order, which become personal superstitions.

It is generally considered unlucky to walk under a ladder, open an umbrella in the house, or break a mirror (which is worth seven years' misfortune). A pinch of spilled salt should be tossed over your left shoulder to avoid bad luck. Killing a spider will cause it to rain the next day.

Omens predicting the future are another aspect of superstition. Some everyday occurrences are considered to have significance. For example, dropping a knife means that company is coming and an itchy palm foretells the acquisition of money. Many people take the need to see the future even further and consult astrologers or fortune-tellers, who read tea leaves, the lines on the palm of a hand, tarot cards or crystal balls to make their prophecies. Fortune-telling leads into the whole area of occult and extra-sensory perception, which is viewed as superstition by some, as a type of science by others.

PLANNING A PARTY

Divide the class into small groups. In your groups, make plans for a party; the party can be wildly imaginary or one the class could actually have. The lists on page 58 give suggestions for types of parties. You can base your parties on Canadian customs and holidays or use some traditions from your native country.

Consider these questions when you plan your party:

When will the party take place (date and time)?
Where will the party take place?
Is the party for a special occasion, such as a birthday or holiday?
Will the party be formal or casual? Is special dress, such as costumes, required?

What kinds of foods and beverages will be served?
Will the guests be required to bring some food or beverages?
Will you have special decorations for the party?
Will there be a theme for the party?

After you have planned your party, make a list of the information that should be given to the guests. (For example, guests would not need to know the menu but would have to be told of a theme in order to dress properly or bring an appropriate gift.) You may wish to practise oral invitations with your group before you invite other class members to your party.

Once your party has been planned, one person from each group should move to a new group and invite its members to the party. The invitations should be kept brief and informal but should include all the information the guests need. The dialogue "A Housewarming" and the dialogue below can be used for examples as to how such a conversation might go. Guests may ask questions about the party and discuss what they plan to bring or wear to the party.

Afterwards, discuss the parties planned by the class. Were any of the plans especially creative? What type of parties do you enjoy? Discuss parties you have attended.

AN INFORMAL INVITATION

A: I was wondering if you would like to come to a skating party that Gillian, Harry and I are having next Friday night.

B: That sounds like fun.

A: There's an outdoor rink in the park near my place. We could meet at my apartment.

C: What time?

A: Eight o'clock okay? And after the skating, we'll have fondue at my place.

C: Okay. Next Friday — is that the eighth?

A: That's right.

D: Only one problem — I don't know how to skate.

A: That's not a problem. I have some extra skates that will probably fit you and we'll teach you.

D: Okay, I'm game for anything once.

TYPES OF PARTIES

Celebrations

birthday
anniversary
house-warming
going away party
retirement
promotion
wedding shower
baby shower
Christmas
New Year
Valentine's Day
Thanksgiving
Easter
Halloween
summer barbecue/picnic
surprise party

Decor or Theme

masquerade
indoor "beach" party
murder mystery
rock 'n roll (fifties nostalgia)
hippies (sixties nostalgia)
children's party
come-as-you-are
a certain colour or object (e.g., a "red" party or a "flower" party)

Food

potluck
coffee and dessert
wine 'n cheese
munchies (chips, pretzels)
buffet
sit-down dinner
finger food (chicken wings, veggies 'n dip)

Additional Vocabulary

do's and don't's guidelines for customs, things one should and should not do

get-together informal social gathering or party

T.G.I.F. "Thank Goodness It's Friday," used at the beginning of the weekend

B.Y.O.B. "Bring Your Own Beverage," an instruction to bring something to drink, such as a bottle of wine or mineral water, to a party

social butterfly someone who has many friends and attends many social engagements

party-pooper, wet blanket (slang) someone who spoils a party by not participating in the fun (a wet blanket puts out a fire)

party animal (slang) someone who enjoys parties very much

crash a party attend a party uninvited

open house party where guests drop in for a short time between the beginning and end time of the party

potluck party dinner where everyone brings a dish

Discussion Topics

1. Describe customs and traditions particular to your culture.
2. What holiday do you enjoy celebrating most? Why?
3. Compare superstitions in Canada to those in your native country. Are you superstitious?
4. What do you think of using omens, astrology or fortune-telling to predict the future?
5. Which Canadian customs do you find different or unusual? Describe any unusual experiences you had when you first learned about these customs.

Additional Activities

1. Give a short oral presentation on a holiday in your native country. Bring items associated with the holiday to show the class.
2. Some regional holidays focus on Canada's heritage, and a national heritage day in February has been proposed. In small groups, plan a new Canadian holiday.

Assignments

1. Consult an etiquette book and newspaper advice columns to find other interesting social do's and don't's.
2. Look up the history and traditions of various holidays in Canada.

8

Love and Marriage

Courtship and Marriage

Courtship and marriage customs vary considerably from culture to culture. In Canada, the customs tend to reflect the diverse ethnic backgrounds in the country; at the same time, many customs described here are characteristic of Canadian weddings in general.

Arranged marriages are rare among Canadians. Most people prefer to get to know members of the opposite sex by going out together. Some may even live together before marrying. If two people decide to get married, they become engaged and the bride-to-be may receive a diamond ring from her **fiancé**. While the parents' permission is not required unless the bride or groom is under legal age, most couples do hope for their parents' approval of the marriage.

Once the couple have set the date, they have many decisions to make — whether they want a large or a small, traditional or non-traditional, civil or church wedding. Weddings also vary in style depending on the ethnic traditions of the bride and groom.

Before the wedding, the bride may be given a number of "showers" by her friends. During these small parties, the bride is "showered" with gifts for the home. Friends of the groom may **throw a bachelor party** before the wedding day. The expense of the wedding itself is traditionally the responsibility of the bride's parents, but today the costs are more likely to be shared by both families and by the bride and groom themselves.

On the day of the wedding, it is considered bad luck for the groom to see the bride before the ceremony. The groom usually wears a **tuxedo** or a formal suit; the bride wears a white gown with a veil. She should have "something old, something new, something borrowed and something blue."

Traditional weddings take place in a church. The groom waits at the altar with the best man. The **ushers** seat the wedding guests. **Bridesmaids** walk up the aisle in a procession followed by the bride, who is accompanied by her father. A minister or priest performs the ceremony and the maid (or matron) of honour and the best man act as official witnesses.

The reception after the ceremony is usually a dinner followed by an evening of dancing. The bride and groom greet their guests in a receiving line. While the guests are seated for the meal, there are speeches and toasts. When the guests **clink** their glasses with silverware, the bride and groom are expected to stand up and kiss each other.

Before the bride and groom leave the reception, they go to all the guests, thanking them and giving them each a piece of wedding cake to take home. The bride throws her **bouquet** to the unmarried women; the woman who catches it is said to be the next to be married. The groom throws the bride's **garter** to the unmarried men. Rice (or **confetti**) thrown at the bride and groom is a symbol of fertility.

Marriages come under provincial **jurisdiction**. A couple must wait at least three days after the licence is obtained to have the ceremony. Judges or marriage commissioners perform civil ceremonies. A civil ceremony is a legal rather than a religious **rite**.

fiancé (m), **fiancée** (f) (Fr.) man or woman (respectively) engaged to be married

to throw a party to give a party

tuxedo (or **tux**) formal suit

usher one who escorts guests to their seats (in theatres, churches); male attendant of the groom

bridesmaids female attendants of the bride

clink to make a short, sharp metallic sound

bouquet bunch of cut flowers

garter band or strap worn to hold up a stocking

confetti small pieces of coloured paper

jurisdiction extent or range of authority

rite ceremony

Discussion

1. List some features of a traditional wedding in Canada.

2. Discuss some other Canadian wedding customs you are familiar with.

3. Compare wedding customs from your native country with the Canadian customs. Discuss ways the customs could be combined for an ethnic wedding in Canada. Have you attended weddings where different ethnic or religious customs have been used?

Going Out

Couples often get to know each other through dating. Typical dates include going out to a movie, to dinner, dancing or to a sports activity. Traditionally, the male asks the female for a date, but this has changed in recent years. In this dialogue, Tanya and Kevin are classmates who meet in the library.

hard at work   to be busy, in the middle of working

finish up   complete, conclude

I've really had it   I've had enough, I'm fed up

looks like   looks as if (this use of "like" is considered ungrammatical in formal English)

take in   attend

pick someone up   call at someone's place, usually to give a ride

Kevin:	**Hard at work**, I see.
Tanya:	Oh, hi Kevin. Are you here doing that sociology paper, too?
Kevin:	Yeah. I'm just **finishing up** the research today — then I can enjoy what's left of the weekend.
Tanya:	I know what you mean. **I've really had it** with this place.
Kevin:	**Looks like** you could use a break. Hey, would you like to go out tonight? I mean, uh, we could **take in** a movie or something. *Citizen Kane* is playing at the Princess.
Tanya:	Really? You know, I've never seen that movie — I've always wanted to since it's supposed to be a classic. I'd love to go.
Kevin:	Great. The early show okay? It's at 7.
Tanya:	Fine.
Kevin:	You live just off campus, don't you?
Tanya:	Yeah, about four blocks from here. I'll give you the address.
Kevin:	I'll **pick you up** around 6:30.
Tanya:	Better make it a little earlier — there's always a line-up at the Princess.
Kevin:	Good idea. I'll see you later, then.
Tanya:	Okay. Bye.

Discussion

1. In what other ways could Kevin have asked Tanya for a date?

2. In pairs, develop and role play a dialogue of a different dating situation. For example, Tanya asks Kevin to come to a dinner party.

3. How do dating customs in Canada differ from those in your country?

4. What do you think is the best way for a couple to get to know each other?

The Perfect Couple

Many explanations have been put forth for the fact that one in three marriages in Canada ends in divorce. While some people argue that a change in traditional marriage roles is the cause of divorce, others point out that today women have the option of choosing divorce over an unhappy marriage. After all, society judges a marriage to be successful simply if it endures, but a society with a low divorce rate cannot necessarily say it has a high rate of good marriages.

Linda: Keith, you'll never believe what's happened!

Keith: What do you mean?

Linda: Monika and Gunnar are getting divorced.

Keith: You're kidding! When? What happened?

Linda: Well, I don't really know, but I heard **through the grapevine** that they've been quietly **separated** for two months already and are filing for divorce. Supposedly, they're still **on speaking terms**.

Keith: That's really surprising — I always thought that they were so **suited to each other**, such similar personalities... What about the kids? Who will get **custody**?

Linda: **Joint custody**, I hear. Apparently it's all quite amicable — no **squabbling** over who'll get the house and stuff. An **uncontested** divorce with all the details worked out.

Keith: Boy, that's a change from all the **back-stabbing** you usually hear about.... I just can't believe it — Monika and Gunnar! The perfect couple.... It just shows you how little one knows about what goes on in people's lives, doesn't it?

---

through the grapevine (idiomatic) through gossip, from other people

separated legally living apart

on speaking terms speaking to each other, not hostile

suited to each other to have similar interests, to be compatible

custody legal responsibility for the care of the children after a divorce

joint custody shared responsibility

squabbling (colloquial) arguing

uncontested not disputed

back-stabbing (colloquial) betrayal, attack

Discussion

1. Why is Keith so surprised?
2. Vary the dialogue by changing the reasons for the divorce and the arrangements. Role play the dialogue variation.
3. Why do you think the divorce rate is so high in modern society?
4. What is necessary for a marriage to be successful?

LANGUAGE NOTES

FRENCH WORDS IN ENGLISH

English has borrowed many words from French. Most borrowings have become anglicized to the point that they are no longer recognizable as French words. Some, however, retain their French spelling (even accent markings) and a modified French pronunciation. French words are often considered elegant and sophisticated; they are especially common in the vocabulary of cooking, dancing and fashion.

In Canada, French words in English are even more important since French is an official language and since most English-speaking Canadians learn French in school. Therefore, English-speaking Canadians are used to hearing and pronouncing French names, as well as the French words that have come into the English language.

The é of the following words is pronounced as /e/, similar to the vowel sound of the English word "say":

fiancé résumé sauté cliché flambé pâté

The following words have the same vowel sound /e/ at the end; the final t is silent:

bouquet ballet buffet parquet

In these words, the eau is pronounced as /ow/, similar to the vowel sound in "rope":

trousseau chateau plateau

The que at the end of a word is pronounced /k/:

boutique mystique critique

In words that come from French, ch is often pronounced like sh /ʃ/:

chef chauvinist chateau champagne

Practise pronunciation of French terms in the following sentences:

1. To make this *pâté*, you must first *sauté* the chicken livers.
2. The chef at the *Chateau* Frontenac is famous for his *flambé* desserts.
3. The suite has *parquet* floors.
4. Our relationship has reached a *plateau*; nothing has changed.
5. The medical profession has a certain *mystique* about it.
6. The *ballet* dancer was very selective at the *buffet* table.
7. I have a *rendezvous* with my *fiancé*.
8. You should have a good *résumé* before you go looking for a job.
9. She is out shopping for her *trousseau* and the bridal *bouquet*.
10. In the sixties, every small shop was called a *boutique*; now that term is a *cliché*.

VERBS WITH "UP"

Up is sometimes added to some verbs to strengthen their meaning. Although the verb can be used alone, up adds the meaning of "completely."

I have to *finish up* this research paper today.
I have enough money *saved* up to buy the television set.
Eat up your vegetables or you won't get any dessert.
The documents *burned up* in the fire.
James *cut up* his credit card into little pieces.
She was in a hurry to *open up* the package.
Heat up the soup before serving.

Compose a sentence for each of the following verbs with and without up, showing the different meanings:

1. read (up)   4. stand (up)
2. clean (up)   5. walk (up)
3. tear (up)   6. dress (up)

DESCRIBING RELATIONSHIPS

People often complain that the English language lacks words that can be used to refer to a person one is dating or living with. "Boyfriend" and "girlfriend" are traditional terms but older adults are uncomfortable using them. People who are engaged can easily refer to their "fiancé" or "fiancée," and married people can refer to their "husband" or "wife." But if a couple are not officially engaged or married, how do they refer to each other?

Attempts have been made to coin new words, but the results have been largely unsuccessful. For example, "POSSLQ" (person of the opposite sex sharing living quarters) never caught on in popularity. So while some people use the understatement "friend" and let listeners come to their own conclusions, others try terms like "partner" and "significant other."

A similar dissatisfaction arises with the term "dating"; it seems old-fashioned today. Therefore, people say they are "going out with" or "seeing" someone.

CULTURE NOTE

The most important change regarding marriage today is that now it is a matter of choice rather than obligation. Part of the choice involves whom to marry (parents had more control over their children's choice of spouse in the past), and part of the choice involves whether to marry at all. Although the vast majority of Canadians (about 90 percent) do marry at some time in their lives, the social, religious and economic pressures to marry or to stay married have lessened.

Traditional marriages have a well-defined division of labour: the husband is the breadwinner and the wife takes care of housekeeping, childcare and related social responsibilities. Today, however, the majority of women are part of the paid labour force and are therefore less dependent on husbands for economic security. Moreover, since society accepts that men should share in domestic and childcare responsibilities, men are no longer viewed as helpless in the home, needing a woman's care. Some, in fact, take over domestic duties entirely.

Married couples enjoy social and financial benefits such as the transfer of income tax deductions and company health plan benefits for a spouse. In many provinces, common-law relationships are treated as marriages; for example, after a breakup there is a formal splitting of property with housework and childcare being counted as contribution to the family income. Gay couples are also demanding such benefits, yet this is still a controversial issue.

In the past, remaining single was viewed as socially unacceptable, especially for women. While the term "bachelor" has the positive connotation of being carefree and enjoying the single life, the corresponding term "spinster" has a negative connotation — an "old maid," someone who is unwanted. Since "Mrs." actually means "married to," women were traditionally known by their husband's name ("Mrs. John Smith"). Today, a variety of naming practices are found. For example, if Jane Doe marries John Smith, she may use Mrs. Jane Smith, Ms. Jane Smith, Ms. Jane Doe-Smith, or Ms. Jane Doe.

Other social changes have affected the divorce rate. For example, with today's greater life expectancy, a couple who marry in their late twenties face 50 years of married life; yet people change and may "grow apart." People also have higher expectations about marriage, including romantic notions fostered by our society's "fairy-tale view" of marriage. As a result, although most Canadians choose marriage, many will agree that no marriage is better than a bad marriage.

AN INTERCULTURAL MARRIAGE

In a multicultural country like Canada, mixed marriages are common. The husband and wife may be from different ethnic groups, religions or races. However, a mixed marriage is not always an intercultural one. For example, second generation immigrants generally follow Canadian cultural traditions and, therefore, have much in common even though their parents may come from very different ethnic groups.

Christine and George met at a Canadian university. He is a foreign student planning to return to his own country. She is a Canadian student. They would like to marry but there are several problems to work out. For example, they have to decide whether to live in her country or his. They have different religions and their cultures have different views of family life. They love each other very much and realize that intercultural marriages have many problems. They also feel willing to work out differences and are open-minded to the viewpoints of other cultures.

George's culture values the traditional patriarchal family. He has been brought up to believe that the husband should be the boss in the family and that the wife should stay home and take care of the children and do the housework. He feels that this is an efficient way to divide up family responsibilities. In his culture, the extended family is very important. Three generations often live together. Adult children follow their parents' judgement in the choice of education, career and spouse. The grandparents have a great deal of control in the raising of their grandchildren.

Christine does not believe that the traditional family is the best arrangement for today's society. She believes that women should participate fully in society and not spend all their time at the home. Her education has prepared her for an interesting career and she thinks that families benefit when both parents have jobs and share the housework and the child-rearing responsibilities. In her culture, it is rare that extended families live together. Children are brought up to be independent and self-sufficient and parents let their adult children make their own decisions.

In small groups, identify potential problem areas for this couple. What do you think they should work out before they marry? Are there compromises that can be made? Do you think the marriage can succeed?

Each group can also make up a dialogue involving the couple and their friends or relatives, showing potential situations. After you work out your dialogue, perform it for the class. For example, you can act out Christine and George talking to their parents or to a marriage counsellor.

Additional Vocabulary

marital status whether a person is single, married, separated, divorced, widowed

blind date a date that is arranged by a third party for two people who are not acquainted

matchmaker, go-between an intermediary, a person who arranges marriages, or introduces prospective brides and grooms

to stand someone up to break a date, not to appear at the appointed time and place

marriage of convenience marriage for legal or social reasons

marriage contract legal agreement between husband and wife outlining domestic responsibilities, marital rights and obligations, and the division of property in the event of a break-up

heterosexual having sexual feelings for a person of the opposite sex

homosexual, gay (m); **lesbian** (f) having sexual feelings for a person of the same sex

Discussion Topics

1. What are the advantages and disadvantages of arranged marriages?

2. Do you think people should live together before getting married?

3. What are the advantages and disadvantages of being married? Of being single?

4. What do you consider acceptable public displays of affection? For example, should couples hold hands in public?

Additional Activities

1. Hold a classroom debate on one of the following topics:

   a) Arranged or traditional marriages are more successful than modern marriages.

   b) Marriage has little meaning in today's society.

   c) Men and women should be equal partners in a marriage.

2. In pairs, develop and role play a dialogue in which a couple deals with a domestic situation such as a financial problem or a problem concerning the children.

Assignments

1. Find out about the laws and regulations concerning marriages at your city hall — for example, the procedure for getting a marriage licence, the cost, the facilities for civil weddings.

2. Look through etiquette books and make a list of wedding traditions. See if you can find the origin for some of these customs.

3. Research separation and divorce laws in your province. Report your findings to the class.

9

Family Ties

Domestic Chores

Different cultures have different approaches to raising children. Canadian parents tend to give children a fair bit of responsibility in order to raise them to be independent adults. For example, children may help around the house, learning to cook and do laundry. In addition, they often receive an allowance and learn to make their own decisions regarding their spending.

The following dialogue takes place during coffee break at nightschool.

Matt: So have you finished the essay for next week yet?

Alina: Are you kidding? I've barely started. Hoped to get some work done on the weekend but I ended up cleaning out the garage. First one thing and then another and before I knew it the weekend was over.

Matt: I know how it is. We did a lot of running around on the weekend — the kids' **swim meet**, shopping, visiting my **folks**. I did get a couple hours' quiet time to work on the paper but I'm still a long way from finished.

Emily: Well, I **for one** don't know how you guys manage taking this night course at all. You've both got full-time jobs as well as family responsibilities. I'm single with only myself to worry about and I still find it **rough**.

Alina: Oh, I don't think I could **hack it** if my kids were still small. But they've gotten to the age where they can help out with a lot of the chores. They even take turns cooking dinner when I've got class and Jacob is working late.

Matt: That sounds great. I can't wait until my kids are old enough to help out more.

Emily: But don't your kids complain about the work? My parents never made me do anything around the house.

Alina: You really have to start them young. When they were **toddlers**, they learned to pick up their toys. And if you get them doing stuff while it's still fun for them they'll get used to it and not think they are being **hard done by**.

Emily: I can't imagine housework being fun for a child.

Matt: But kids love doing **grown up** stuff. My oldest daughter loves to scrub the bathtub. We use baking soda and she thinks it's great fun to splash around in the water. The tub doesn't get perfectly clean but she's learning.

Emily: Yeah, I guess so. Maybe if I'd had to do more around the house when I was young, it wouldn't've been so hard to learn when I got my own place.

swim meet swimming competition

folks (slang) parents

for one (emphatic expression) myself

rough difficult

hack it (slang) do it, manage

toddlers young children between the ages of one and three who have learned to walk but are still rather unsteady

hard done by (informal) unfairly treated

grown up adult

Discussion

1. What advantages and disadvantages of having children do housework are mentioned or implied in this dialogue? Can you think of others?

2. What do you think of children having to do housework? Did you have to do any? Do (or will) your children?

3. What are suitable chores for young children to do?

4. What is the ideal way for chores to be split among family members?

5. Discuss different approaches to raising children.

The Generation Gap

As children approach adulthood, they often find that they feel differently from their parents on a number of issues. This difference is called the generation gap. This phenomenon is not limited to the present time; ancient Roman documents show that parents worried about their children not following traditional ways. Immigrant families may find this difference is made even greater by a culture gap; their children are learning the ways of the new culture and may find it even more difficult to accept their parents' views.

on the home front at home

UBC University of British Columbia

last ditch effort (idiom) final attempt before defeat, last place that can be defended

U of A University of Alberta

baby of the family (informal) youngest child

headstrong determined to do what she wants despite others' advice

black sheep one that does not fit into the group, rebel

put her foot down (idiom) insisted

empty-nesters (idiom) parents whose children have grown-up and left home (the nest)

Ning: And how's everything going **on the home front**?

Kaz: Not too bad. Things are a little quieter these days now that Magda's off at university.

Ning: So she went to **UBC** after all.

Kaz: Yeah, Teresa made a **last ditch effort** to convince her to go to **U of A** instead, but Magda insisted that she wanted to live away from home now and that UBC had the best program for her.

Ning: She's going to be in residence anyway, so it's not like she'll be completely on her own. You just worry about her because she's the **baby of the family**.

Kaz: I guess. But she's so **headstrong**. She reminds me so much of my brother. And he was really the **black sheep** of our family.

Ning: A black sheep? Just because he didn't go into the family business?

Kaz: My father took it pretty hard. Thought it was a defection.

Ning: Well, you should've seen the commotion at our place a few years ago when my daughter went off to university. My mother insisted that an education is no use to a woman, that Rose should just get married and have a family.

Kaz: You're lucky she didn't try to arrange a marriage for her.

Ning: Oh she tried. But Rose **put her foot down** and said no way was she going to talk to any matchmaker.

Kaz: That must've been quite the scene.

Ning: Yeah, and my mother still isn't happy now that Rose is married and has children. She complains the kids don't know enough Chinese and she has trouble talking to them.

Kaz: I remember how hard it was for me when my kids started school and learned to speak English better than me. And they had to correct my spelling all the time, even for notes to the teacher.

Ning: But now they're grown and you and Teresa are **empty-nesters**. Enjoy the freedom.

Discussion

1. In your own words, explain the family conflicts mentioned in this conversation.
2. Discuss these conflicts and any similar ones you have experienced.
3. What do you think of the generation gap? Is it worse or better for immigrant families?

LANGUAGE NOTES

COLOURS

The link between colours and emotions is well-established. For example, there is the distinction between "warm" colours (red, orange, brown) and "cool" colours (blue, green). Red is a powerful, strong colour and implies strong emotion, such as passion, warning ("a red flag") or anger (e.g., to "see red" means to be angry). In old movies "the good guy" usually wore white, while the villain wore black. The negative associations of black can be seen in such expressions as a "black look" and "blacklist," although being "in the black" (operating at a profit) is positive.

Sometimes cultures can use colours quite differently. For example, in Chinese tradition white is the colour of mourning and red the colour of happiness, so a bride usually wears red. A Canadian bride, in contrast, wears a white dress to represent purity. A red dress would imply promiscuity (as in the old phrase, "a scarlet woman").

Another traditional use of colours in Canada is for baby clothes. Pink is traditionally used for girls and light blue for boys. However, some people object to this type of gender typing.

The names of some colours are used to describe people in terms of their emotions:

> She's been feeling *blue* since she didn't get the promotion. (sad, depressed)
> Martin was practically *green* when I showed him my new sports car. (envious, jealous)
> I'm still very *green* at this so you'll have to give me a hand. (inexperienced)
> The soldiers accused them of being *yellow*, but I think they were just being prudent. (cowardly)

Idioms and expressions also use colour words:

> I try to buy *green* products whenever I can. (environmentally safe)
> That's still a *grey area* in our plans but we're waiting to see the new legislation *in black and white*. (unclear, not definite; in writing)
> *Once in a blue moon*, they rent a *blue* movie. (infrequently, rarely; an erotic or pornographic film)
> The company *put out the red carpet* for the visitors from Japan. (welcomed the visitors as if they were royalty)
> They caught the embezzler *red-handed*. (in the act of the crime)
> I always end up telling her *white lies* in order to spare her feelings. (small lies that are often told in social situations)

PARTICIPLES

The present and past participle of some verbs are often confused. The present participle is the active form of the regular verb. The past participle is the passive form. This distinction is important to remember; confusing the participles may be misleading and even humorous. "I am boring" (present participle), for example, does not mean the same as "I am bored" (past participle).

Compare the different meanings in the following examples:

> I am interested in stamp collecting.
> Stamp collecting is interesting to me.
> (Stamp collecting interests me.)

> I am bored with this class.
> This class is boring.
> (This class bores me.)

> I am confused about this subject.
> This subject is confusing.
> (This subject confuses me.)

> I am excited about going on this trip.
> This trip will be very exciting.

> I am very tired.
> My day was very tiring.

CULTURE NOTE

Families in Canada can take very different forms. Some are traditional nuclear families while others are large extended families. Some are single-parent families and others are couples with no children. In some families, sex roles follow the traditional pattern of a breadwinner father and a stay-at-home mother; in others, work and family responsibilities are divided according to talent and opportunity. Different ethnic traditions also influence family structure and family life in Canada.

Since so many Canadians came as immigrants to the country, they often had to leave their extended families behind. Moreover, Canadian society is a very mobile one; adult children, grandparents, aunts, uncles and cousins often live in different cities, or even different provinces. As a result, Canadians do not have a strong tradition of living together with extended family.

Recent social changes have had an impact on family life. The birth rate has fallen; it is now about 1.7 children per couple. Since a birth rate of 2.1 is needed to keep a population stable, immigration is encouraged to ensure Canada's growth.

Another major change is that the majority of Canadian families have both parents in the workforce, even when children are pre-school age. Although fathers are taking on more childcare responsibilities and doing more housework than they traditionally did in the past, statistics show that mothers still do the lion's share of this work. Families tend to have less leisure time than they did in the past.

Divorce has also caused change in family structure. Although the divorce rate in Canada is considered alarmingly high, it must be remembered that a low divorce rate does not necessarily mean a high rate of successful marriages. Since divorces are now easier to obtain, both legally and socially, couples may choose to divorce rather than to stay in an unhappy marriage.

After a divorce, children usually live with their mothers, although fathers who fight for custody of children in court do tend to win. Even though non-custodial fathers pay child support and sometimes alimony, statistics show that the standard of living of the father tends to improve after divorce and that the mother and the children suffer economically.

Modern family situations can be extremely confusing after marriage breakdowns and re-marriages. Today's children can live in blended families with step-parents, step-brothers and step-sisters. If their parents have joint custody, they may also have two homes.

The family is the basic unit of society and cultural values are passed on from parent to child. In some cultures, teenage and adult children are expected to follow the wishes of their parents in choices of education, career and spouse. Canadians, however, generally value independence in adults. As a result, children are brought up to learn responsibility so that they can make their own decisions. Many young adults leave their family home between the age of 18 and 23 and live on their own or with their peers.

Elderly parents also prefer to live independently, if their health permits it. The children often find it difficult to take an elderly parent into their own home, especially when they are working and cannot stay home to provide care. In Canada, many elderly people live in nursing homes or homes for the elderly and are supported by social security.

With families being such an important part of society, gov-ernment and business have to deal with many family issues and take care of some of the responsibilities traditionally assigned to stay-at-home mothers. Taking care of children, the sick and the elderly are obvious areas where institutions now play a larger part. Social benefits such as unemployment insurance and pensions also mean that people are less dependent on their families today.

FAMILY COURT — CUSTODY HEARING

Role play a custody hearing with students playing the parts of characters described below. Other characters can be added to act as witnesses. Alternative scenarios are also given. You can change or add to the situations, if you wish, or make up some of your own scenarios.

Alternatively, you can use the situation below as a problem-solving activity and group discussion. Who do you think should get custody? Discuss different aspects of the situation and list possible solutions. Compare the different scenarios.

SITUATION

Alan Starr and Claire Molina were married for ten years and they have been divorced for three years. The children have been living with their mother and spend occasional weekends and holidays with

their father. Alan Starr pays child support but does not pay alimony. Now Starr has remarried; his new wife has a five-year old child. He wants to change the custody arrangement so that the children would come and live with him.

MAIN CHARACTERS

Alan Starr is a successful businessman. When he was married to his first wife, he did not spend much time with the children. He is a hardworking executive and travels frequently. However, he expects to be promoted to a job that will require less travel.

Claire Molina is a bookkeeper with a moderate income. She stayed at home until her second child started school. She works full time and the children go to a babysitter for two hours after school. However, she spends a lot of time with her children in the evenings and during the weekends.

Alicia Khan-Starr is Alan Starr's second wife. She has a part-time job as a store clerk and assumes most of the housekeeping and childcare responsibilities. She has never been married before; she was a single mother to her five-year old daughter, Tiffany.

The children of Alan Starr and Claire Molina are **Brandon**, ten years old, and **Jessica**, eight years old. They have adjusted fairly well to the divorce. The biggest change for them is a drop in lifestyle; they had to move from a larger home to a smaller one.

OTHER CHARACTERS

Judge **Sylvie Nguyen**
John Lawson, the lawyer for Claire Molina
Max Ohta, the lawyer for Alan Starr
Witnesses — other characters can be added as character witnesses (such as friends and neighbours) or professional witnesses (such as a school psychologist or social worker)

ALTERNATIVE SCENARIOS

These are alternative scenarios for a first hearing to award custody of the children.

1. Neither partner has remarried. Starr is a writer who works at home and therefore handles much of the childcare responsibilities. Molina works for an ad agency in an executive position; she must travel frequently. Both want custody of the children.

2. Instead of being a divorced father, Starr is a widower, who has a full-time job but is home most evenings and weekends with his children. His late wife's parents, who are retired and therefore at home all day, want custody of the children.

3. Molina is remarrying and her future husband lives in another country. She wants to take the children with her, but Starr objects. Both Molina and Starr have full-time jobs away from home.

Additional Vocabulary

peers individuals of the same age and social group

adolescent teenager in the state of growth from childhood to maturity

only child child without any brothers or sisters

siblings brothers and sisters

senior citizen individual over the age of 65

alimony payment made to one spouse by another after divorce

child support after-divorce payment made for children's expenses

Discussion Topics

1. Discuss family life in Canada and in your native countries.

2. What are the advantages and disadvantages of sharing a home with extended family?

3. If your elderly parents needed a place to live, would you offer your home? Why or why not? What are the advantages and disadvantages?

4. What do you think of fathers being present when their children are born?

5. "Sibling rivalry" refers to the problems brothers and sisters often have in getting along. What are some common problems? Did you experience these kinds of difficulties? Do you have any suggestions for parents to minimize sibling rivalry?

6. Some psychologists say that birth order influences personality. For example, first-borns are often independent and have good leadership qualities. Last-born children are often spoiled and used to being babied. Do you agree with this idea? What is your experience?

7. Discuss some of the childhood stories well-known in your culture.

Additional Activities

1. Hold a classroom debate on one of the following topics:
   a) Mothers should not work outside the home.
   b) Children should look after their elderly parents rather than send them to institutions.
   c) Adoption records should be open so that children can find their natural parents.

2. Role play the following dialogues:
   a) parents discussing their child's discipline problems at school;
   b) a teenager asking a parent to use the car;
   c) a couple checking out a day-care centre;
   d) an elderly couple deciding whether to live with their children or in a home for the elderly;
   e) a middle-aged man telling his wife he wants to change his career;
   f) a middle-aged woman discussing her plans to return to school.

3. In small groups, make a list of rules or guidelines that you think parents should follow when they raise children.

Assignments

1. Look up statistics concerning families in Canada (e.g., average number of children per family, number of single-parent families) and report your findings to the class.

2. Make a list of the households you know according to family units, such as nuclear families, groups of single people sharing accommodations, or extended families living together. Compare your list with your classmates and discuss your findings.

Home Sweet Home

débris = litter, garbage.
competitive

Home Sweet Home   77

House Hunting

Home ownership is the goal of many Canadian families. Many view it as a long-term investment, especially when the mortgage is paid off by retirement. Government-sponsored incentive programmes have included tax-free savings plans to encourage people to save for a house.

Midori: Sorry I'm late, Karen. It took a bit longer at the library than I **figured**.

Karen: Oh, that's okay. I'm running late today myself. I just started getting lunch ready. Did you get anything interesting at the library?

Midori: A couple books on buying a house.

Karen: A house? I thought you and Jim were going to wait a couple more years to buy a house.

Midori: We were. But now that interest rates have fallen and we've managed to get some money saved for a **down-payment** ... well, it seems like a good time to buy.

Karen: It does look like a **buyer's market** right now. Which part of town are you interested in?

Midori: That's the dilemma. I'd like to live near the university and renovate an older house.

Karen: But that part of town is **trendy** now. People are **flocking** to it and the prices are really going up.

Midori: That's what Jim says. He'd prefer a house in one of the new **subdivisions**. We could get a bigger house for the same amount of money.

Karen: And they have all the modern conveniences — extra bathrooms, family rooms.

Midori: But they lack the character of an older place. And I don't want to live **in the sticks** and have to **commute** to work each day.

Karen: Well, maybe you two will reach some sort of compromise.

Midori: I suppose so. In the end, it will all depend on our bank account.

Karen: Funny how the **bottom line** is always the deciding factor.

figured (colloquial) thought, estimated

down-payment part of the full price paid at delivery or purchase time, with the rest made up in monthly payments

buyer's market good market for buyers (as opposed to a seller's market, when there is more demand than supply)

trendy fashionable

flock (idiomatic) gather in a large group, crowd together (used metaphorically — birds travel in a flock)

subdivisions new residential developments

in the sticks (slang) far from the centre of town, in the suburbs or a rural area

commute travel a long distance from home to work, often from one community to another

bottom line the result in a budget, the total figure giving profit or loss

Discussion

1. Where and when is this conversation taking place?
2. What have Midori and Jim changed their minds about and why?
3. Summarize the advantages and disadvantages of a house in the suburbs and one in the city core. Where would you prefer to live?

Moving Out

University and college students face difficult decisions about living accommodation. For many it is the first time they will live away from their families. School residences offer the convenience of being on campus and the opportunity to socialize with other students. Often students choose residence for their first year when they are new to the city.

Arctic sovereignty political issue concerning control of waterways between the islands in Canada's north

wanna reduced spoken form of "want to"

geez exclamation of wonderment

getting to me bothering me

racket loud noise

zoo (slang) wild place

yuck exclamation of disgust

didn't sound half bad (colloquial) sounded quite good

it'll cost a mint (colloquial) it will be very expensive

scrounge hunt up, look for

garage sales private sales in garages where people sell used articles they no longer want

thrift shops second-hand stores

sounds like sounds as if (ungrammatical use of "like" often heard in informal English)

work cut out a lot of work to do

David: Whew! I thought that class would never end.

Pavel: Yeah, once Sorenson starts talking about **Arctic sovereignty**, he never shuts up. I'm going back to my room for a coffee — **wanna** join me?

David: Sounds good. **Geez**, you're lucky to have a place right on campus like this.

Pavel: I used to think so. But after two years, residence life is **getting to me**. It was great in first year 'cause I got to meet people. But I'm getting tired of the **racket** — our lounge can be a real **zoo**.

David: Yeah, but it is convenient. And you don't have to cook your own meals...

Pavel: You try living on cafeteria food for a while — **yuck**!... and anyway, what are you talking about — you live at home, you get all your meals home-cooked.

David: Living at home can be a hassle too. My brothers and sisters are a lot younger than I am — you can imagine. I've been thinking of moving out. It'd be worth the expense just to get some independence.

Pavel: It's not so expensive if you have a roommate.

David: Hey — why not? I saw some ads for apartments that **didn't sound half bad**.

Pavel: But what about furniture and dishes? **It'll cost a mint** just to get set up.

David: I bet my parents would let me have some of the old stuff in the basement. And we could **scrounge** around for some other things — **garage sales**, **thrift shops**.

Pavel: **Sounds like** we've got our **work cut out for us** — let's go get a paper and look through some ads.

Discussion

1. What is the relationship between David and Pavel?

2. What are the advantages and disadvantages of living in a student residence? Of having an apartment? Of living with your parents?

3. In groups of three, develop and role play a conversation between Pavel (or David) and his parents concerning his plans for a place of his own.

4. In small groups, make a list of criteria for David and Pavel's apartment. Using the classified ads in the newspaper, choose a likely apartment and role play phone calls and apartment viewings.

5. In small groups, pretend that you are going to become roommates. Make a list of what you will need. Decide on where you are going to live, what each person will contribute, and the domestic and financial responsibilities each person will have.

LANGUAGE NOTES

COMPARISONS

Various comparisons can be used to describe people and things. The comparative and superlative forms of adjectives and adverbs are formed by using *more* and *most* or the endings -er and -est. The definite article is used with the superlative form:

This book is more expensive than that one.
He runs faster than Jennifer.
That is the most outrageous statement I have ever heard.
He is the tallest boy in the class.

Confusion is sometimes caused by the difference between *than* and *then*. In sentences, the two words sound exactly the same because they are unstressed function words and the vowel sound of *than* is reduced. However, *than* is used for comparisons and *then* is an adverb of time:

That car is more expensive *than* I imagined.
I delivered the package and *then* I left.

When people are compared, the subject form of the pronoun is used in formal English:

Marjorie is younger than I am.
Cathy has more money than he.

In informal English, however, the object form of the pronoun is acceptable and is often heard in speech:

She plays better than him.
Elizabeth swims as fast as me.

The pattern *as ... as* is used to compare things of equal value:

Matthew is as clever as his sister.
This story is not as interesting as that one.

In informal English, *like* is often used instead of the proper *as* in comparisons and similes:

You look like you've been up all night.
(You look as if you've been up all night.)
He acts like he knows the way.
(He acts as if he knows the way.)

Compose sentences comparing:

1. rural and urban lifestyles;
2. living in small and large houses;
3. renting and owning accommodation;
4. living in an apartment and house;
5. lifestyles in Canada and in your culture.

ANIMAL METAPHORS AND SIMILES

References to animals appear in many expressions and idioms in English. A simile is a direct comparison made with *like* or *as*, while a metaphor is a comparison that is not stated in the comparative form. Verbs describing animal behaviour can be used as colourful descriptions of human actions.

One type of animal metaphor is made from the words for animal groups. Different types of animals have different words to describe their groups, and some of these group words have a corresponding verb form. For example:

a flock of birds, to flock
a herd of cattle, to herd
a swarm of insects, to swarm
a school of fish
a pack of wolves

These verb forms can be applied to people, to show actions that are similar to the animals':

The enthusiastic fans *swarmed* around the rock star.
The classroom monitor *herded* the students out when the fire alarm sounded.
Families are *flocking* to that new amusement park.

Words describing animal sounds can also be used for human behaviour:

The drill sergeant barked out the orders. (dogs bark)
Excited about the new activities, the children buzzed around the classroom. (bees buzz)
The child's mother clucked her disapproval when she saw him covered with mud. (hens cluck)
He's a nice guy, but I hate it when he starts crowing about his achievements. (roosters crow)

Certain animal characteristics are used in similes to describe people:

blind as a bat   proud as a peacock
busy as a bee   slippery as an eel
crazy as a loon   quiet as a mouse
free as a bird   weak as a kitten
gentle as a lamb   wise as an owl
happy as a lark

USE OF "HOUSE"/"HOME"

While *house* and *home* are synonymous, differences in usage of the two words should be noted. While *house* generally refers to a single-family dwelling, *home* is used for any type of dwelling or for a geographical location (e.g., "I'm going home for the holidays"). *Home* carries an emotional connotation (which is why real estate agents often advertise "homes for sale").

House does not always refer to a separate building. It is used in such expressions as: "to keep house," "to set up house," "household," "housekeeper," "housework." It can be used to refer to a business ("a publishing house") and to people within a building (e.g., "He woke the whole house up"). "In-house" is used to describe something kept within a certain company or group of people, such as "an in-house investigation."

Home is used without a preposition in such phrases as: "come home," "stay home," "go home," "be home," "walk home," "leave home." When there is no movement, "at home" is used.

Note also the difference between "housework" (cleaning the house) and "homework" (school work brought home to do).

Idioms with *House* and *Home*

The restaurant owner said to his friend, "You'll have to come in and see the new place. Bring some friends and I'll cook a special dinner — *on the house*, of course." (free, paid for by the establishment)

This new job title may sound impressive, but it's really *nothing to write home about*. (not special or impressive)

When I arrived at the apartment, she told me *to make myself at home*. (to make myself comfortable, to act as if it were my home)

During the recession, his business was like *a house of cards*. (an unstable structure)

The police officer's warnings about drinking and driving really *hit home* with the teenagers when they thought about their friend's accident. (had an effect, became a realization)

Only a couple more weeks of term — we're *in the home stretch* now. (near the goal, almost finished)

The performance was so electrifying that it *brought the house down*. (caused loud applause from the audience)

CULTURE NOTE

Many Canadians enjoy the luxury of a large amount of living space. Canada is vast, and the homes are large according to the standards of many countries. Even crowded inner cities do not reach the extremes found in other parts of the world.

Canadians appreciate the space and value their privacy. Since families are generally small, many Canadian children enjoy the luxury of their own bedroom. In fact, there is a tendency towards having a separate play area for children and a

retreat-like master bedroom for the parents, containing a sitting area and an en suite bathroom.

Many rooms in Canadian homes have specialized functions. Family rooms are popular features in modern houses; these are, in fact, living rooms since

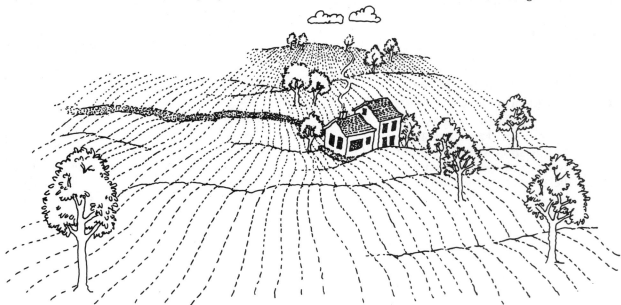

many "living rooms" have become reserved for entertaining. Some homes have a formal dining area in addition to an eat-in kitchen that is used for casual family meals.

Recreational homes are also popular with Canadians. Some Canadians own summer homes, often called "cottages," which are located in the country, in the mountains or near a lake. These may be small one-room cabins or houses with all the conveniences and comforts of home.

Changes in lifestyle in Canadian society have resulted in changes in home life. For instance, increased mobility has meant that people do not feel rooted in their neighbourhood and may not get to know their neighbours. Moreover, fewer hours are spent at home because of such factors as long work hours, commuting time and participation in courses or leisure activities. (In the past, women spent most of their time at home and therefore made contact with other women in the neighbourhood.) As a result, people are more isolated in their homes and have less community spirit.

However, a recognition of the value of home life can be seen in the trend toward home offices. Commuting to work is both time- and energy-consuming. Developments in technology have created communications tools such as computers with modems, fax machines and multi-feature telephones, which have made keeping in touch with clients and co-workers easy. As a result, some people run their own businesses from their homes and others spend some part of their week working at home.

More emphasis on family activities also improves the quality of Canadian home-life. For instance, the term "cocooning" was coined in the late 1980s to refer to staying at home for entertainment — renting a movie for the VCR, making popcorn, playing board games with the children and ordering take-out food. Canadians are finding the truth in such old sayings as "Home is where the heart is."

DESCRIBING YOUR HOME

Working in pairs, describe the layout of your home to your partner, who will draw a sketch of the layout while you are talking. Your partner may wish to ask questions to clarify the description. Afterwards, check your partner's sketch for accuracy. You can then change roles, with the other student describing while you sketch.

For your home, you can choose to describe the layout of a room, a floor, the building or even the neighbourhood. You can describe the home you are living in now, one you have lived in or your "dream home."

EXAMPLE 1

"My home is a two-bedroom apartment. When you come in the door, you are in a long hallway that goes to the left. To the right is the living room. It has windows along the east wall and a small eating area near the south wall. Straight ahead is a large kitchen with windows on the north wall. The closet is to the left of the entrance to the kitchen. If you turn left and go down the hall you pass first the door to the bathroom, then the first bedroom. The door to the second bedroom is at the end of the hall."

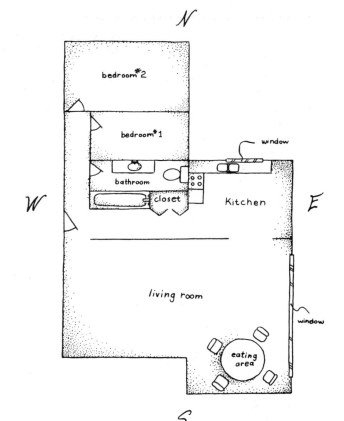

EXAMPLE 2

"I live in a room in the university residence. It is a long, rectangular room with a door at one end and a window at the other. As you enter the room, first there is a closet on the left side near the door. Along the left wall is the bed with a bookcase headboard at the window wall. Near the window on the right hand side of the room is an armchair. Next to it is a desk with a bulletin board hanging over it. Next to the desk, near the door, is a bookcase."

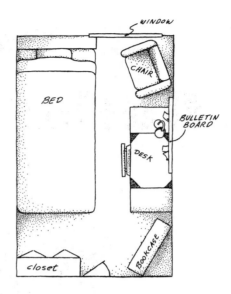

Additional Vocabulary

landlord someone who lets or rents out property to a tenant; owner of a building

high-rise building with more than 12 storeys

walk-up building with no elevator, usually up to five storeys

condo (condominium) apartment or townhouse that is owned rather than rented; owner usually pays fees to cover maintenance of building and property

mortgage claim on property given to a individual, bank or firm for money loaned; loan on a property

Note: Terms for different kinds of buildings may vary from region to region, and even city to city, in Canada. In some places, a "duplex" is a building that contains two apartments; in others, it is two houses joined with one common wall. Another example is the use of the word "suite" for an apartment in Alberta; in other areas, such as Ontario, "suite" is used to describe more than one room together in a hotel, but not an apartment.

Discussion Topics

1. Discuss the merits of renting and of owning accommodation.
2. What factors are important when you look for a place to live?
3. Do you prefer city or country living?

4. How do Canadian homes differ from those in your country? How does the type of home affect lifestyle?
5. What do you like and dislike about your neighbourhood?
6. What does it take to be a good neighbour?
7. What are the advantages and disadvantages of working at home?

Additional Activities

1. In a group, go through the real estate section of your local newspaper. Try to get an idea of the market in your city. Compare the different areas of the city. What kind of rental accommodation is available? What are the costs?
2. Using real estate advertising, make a list of terms used to describe dwellings.
3. Examine floor plans of houses and apartments to compare the layouts of Canadian living space with homes in your native country.
4. In small groups, develop and role play a dialogue of a real estate agent with clients, or of a landlord and a tenant discussing problems.

Assignments

1. Find out about the landlord-tenant laws in your area. Look at various rental applications.
2. Research the community services in your neighbourhood and report your findings to the class.

11
Hitting the Books

Continuing Ed

Adult education courses are offered by most school boards, colleges and universities. These can be upgrading, special certificate or general interest courses. They are usually given by a separate department from the regular credit courses. While most are given in the evening, there are also some daytime or weekend classes.

what'cha doin? (informal) reduction of "What are you doing?"

wine appreciation wine tasting, a course to learn about different kinds of wine

can't get anywhere can't make progress or be promoted

dead-end job job with no future prospects, no hope of promotion

chef extraordinaire (Fr.) extraordinary chef, great professional cook (used sarcastically in the dialogue)

now you're talking (colloquial) that's a good idea

Paul:	**What'cha doin'?**
Ali:	I'm just trying to decide between a computer course or an accounting course.
Paul:	You goin' back to school?
Ali:	I was just thinking of taking a night course.
Paul:	Why would you want to waste perfectly good evenings sitting at a desk?
Ali:	I don't think they're wasted. I enjoy night courses — you learn new skills, meet new people. Last year I took a **wine appreciation** course.
Paul:	Now that sounds like a good class. But why accounting? Or computers?
Ali:	I **can't get anywhere** at the office — I've got a **dead-end job.** I figure some new skills might help.
Paul:	(looking in the brochure) Hmm... there are some good courses here — Photography, Investing in Real Estate, Public Speaking and all kinds of languages.
Ali:	So, why don't you take a course too?
Paul:	I just might do that. Here's some cooking courses.
Ali:	Oh, yeah, I can just see it — Paul Barker — **chef extraordinaire.**
Paul:	No, I'm serious. They have one here especially for beginners. I'm getting tired of take-out food and microwave frozen dinners.
Ali:	Hey, you know, those cooking classes might be a great way to meet new people — especially girls.
Paul:	**Now you're talking.**

Discussion

1. What is Ali's opinion of night courses? And Paul's? How does Paul's opinion change?

2. What is your opinion of adult education? What kind of courses would you like to take?

3. What is the adult education department at your school called? In groups, take a look at various brochures for adult education and discuss the different courses offered.

ESL Class

Adults going back to school often find they have to make adjustments. For instance, it may be years since they had to read intensively or write essays. Assignment deadlines may be hard to meet, especially when school is only a small part of a busy week. Some adults associate schoolwork with childhood and feel that they are too old to be in class again, especially if the teacher is younger than they are. Moreover, students who received their education in a different country may have difficulty adjusting to Canadian instructional methods. Despite these difficulties, adults often find going back to school rewarding.

Sophie: So, how are your English classes going, Ivan?

Ivan: Not too bad. It's **funny** being back in school, though. I haven't had to do homework in years.

Sophie: You think it's helping you?

Ivan: Oh, yeah. I picked up my English here and there, you know. I never really studied it in school.

Sophie: Really? You speak English so well.

Ivan: But my writing is really terrible. And if I want to change my job, I need to write English well. My teacher says I'm really improving, though.

Sophie: What's your teacher like?

Ivan: Very nice. He seems so young, though. Or maybe it's just because I feel so old sitting in a classroom.

Sophie: Are all the students young, then?

Ivan: Oh, no. There's one guy who must be close to seventy. And he keeps **plugging away**.

Sophie: Maybe there's not so much truth in that old proverb, **"You can't teach an old dog new tricks."**

Ivan: It's hard getting used to this kind of school. I remember school being so strict — everybody sitting in rows quietly doing drills and exercises. Our classroom is so relaxed that people talk without raising their hands.

Sophie: Well, I think it's good you're going to school like that. Just the thought of facing a teacher again gives me **cold feet**.

Ivan: Oh, it's not so bad. It helps that all students are **in the same boat** — we're all adults back in school to improve our English.

funny   strange, unusual (the two uses of the word "funny" in English are sometimes cleared up by the question "You mean funny ha-ha or funny strange?")

plugging away   (slang) working hard

You can't teach an old dog new tricks   (proverb) as people get older they are less likely to learn new things

cold feet   (colloquial) "to have cold feet" means to be afraid of doing something

in the same boat   (idiomatic) in the same situation

Discussion

1. Describe Ivan's English in your own words.
2. Why is he studying English?
3. How do you feel about studying English?
4. How are your classes different from school in your native country?

LANGUAGE NOTES

"YOU" AS AN INDEFINITE PRONOUN

In casual speech, the pronoun *you* is frequently used instead of *one* as an indefinite pronoun, meaning people in general. It is considered more friendly and much less formal than *one*. Compare these examples:

> You can take English classes in the daytime or in the evening.
> One must be careful crossing that street.

This use of the pronoun *you* is also common in proverbs and other expressions such as, "you'd better watch out for..."

> Proverb: You can lead a horse to water but you can't make him drink. (You can show someone what is good, but that does not mean that he or she will take advantage of it.)

In writing, the use of *you* as an indefinite pronoun is considered incorrect; either the pronoun *one* or an alternate construction, such as the passive, must be used. For example:

> One must begin the process again.
> This article must be read carefully.

In the common expression "you know," *you* is sometimes used as a general pronoun. The expression can be used in several different ways. It can be a hesitation marker:

> It's close to that new restaurant — umm, you know — what's the name of the place again?

It is also used to introduce a new fact:

> You know, that place closed down last week.

It can also be used as a request for agreement:

> They really are the best team in the league, you know.

Some people use this expression excessively so that it becomes a verbal tic (involuntary repetition).

REDUCTION OF SOUNDS

Many verbal expressions, especially those with auxiliary verbs, are reduced in everyday spoken English — "I dunno," for example. Although it is not necessary for those learning English to use these reduced forms, it is important to be able to understand them.

Vowel sounds are omitted and consonant sounds are merged in the process of contraction and ellipsis (omission of words or sounds). These reductions occur only in speech, but written forms are used in dialogues or plays to show the pronunciation. Compare these examples:

I don't know	I dunno
have got to	gotta
going to	gonna
want to	wanna
have to	hafta
supposed to	s'posed to
ought to	oughta
could have	coulda

Other informal reduced forms include:

What are you doing?	What'cha doin?
How did you do it?	How'dja do it?
I had better go now.	I better go now.

ANATOMICAL IDIOMS

In the dialogue "ESL Class," Sophie refers to having "cold feet." Many idioms and expressions in English refer to parts of the body, such as the following examples:

> I'm afraid our partnership is not going too well; we just can't *see eye-to-eye* on so many issues. (agree)
> Tell me the story now — I'm *all ears*. (listening with full attention)
> That story was told *tongue in cheek*. (not seriously)
> The name was *on the tip of my tongue*, but I just can't remember it. (almost remembered)
> That good evaluation was a *shot in the arm* for her. (encouragement)
> I finally managed to get that bathroom clean. It just took a lot of *elbow grease*. (physical effort)
> I've got to *hand it to you* — you did a good job on that report. (congratulate you)
> They called someone in from the computer department but she couldn't *put her finger on* exactly what was causing the problem. (find out, determine precisely)
> You'd better tell them to *shake a leg* or we'll be late. (hurry up)
> They'll have to be *on their toes* if they want to win. (alert, attentive)

CULTURE NOTE

In Canada, education falls under provincial jurisdiction, so schooling varies from province to province. The situation is further complicated by the fact that each province may have a public school system, a separate school system (Roman Catholic schools), French and English schools, and other schools determined by religious denominations. Moreover, curriculum and school operations are controlled by a school board in each region or city. There are also private schools which receive little or no government funding. In addition, parents may choose to educate their children at home instead of in school, but they must meet education ministry curriculum requirements and follow guidelines.

Despite the lack of uniformity among Canadian schools, some general characteristics are apparent. School is compulsory for children from about the age of 6 to 16. Most students exceed this minimum requirement by attending kindergarten when they are 5 years old and by graduating from high school when they are about 18. Students in elementary school follow a curriculum starting from basic reading and arithmetic skills in Grade 1. In secondary school, students start choosing courses to specialize their education. For example, students who are academically inclined choose courses that will eventually lead them to university.

Post-secondary schools include colleges and universities. Usually, colleges are vocationally oriented, training people for specific jobs. Universities offer wider-based academic studies, as well as training for various professions (law, medicine, teaching, engineering, etc.). While students do pay tuition fees for post-secondary education, most of the costs of colleges and universities are borne by the government.

In addition to meeting the requirements set by the government, the Canadian education system must answer to parents and to employers' demands for a workforce. Moreover, the Canadian school population is not a homogeneous one and individual students require different types of education. The school system must respond to the needs of students with differing abilities and interests as well as students from different cultures, speaking other languages.

Meeting the needs of different students is more complicated when everyone seems to have a different opinion of what a good education is. Some people favour traditional learning with an emphasis on the memorization of facts. However, this approach is viewed as inadequate in view of the glut of information in today's world. Students need to develop the skills required for finding information, digesting it and evaluating it.

With all these issues on the agenda, Canadian schools find that individualized instruction and cooperative learning are good ways to meet different students' needs. For example, traditional Grade 1 reading instruction had all the students learning to read from the same textbook, page by page. Today, instead of a textbook, students choose which books to read, practising reading aloud with the teacher or another student, and doing a report on their book. Cooperative learning involves students working on projects or problems as a group with peer help as well as guidance from the teacher. Active learning — learning by doing rather than learning by listening — is stressed. Students do independent research projects, solve problems and form opinions. Classroom activity is based on the discussion of ideas.

POST-SECONDARY CHOICES

Angela has just finished high school. She has good marks, especially in math and languages. She is currently living in a large city with her family. She has no specific career goals in mind but the ideas of working with computers, teaching or working as an interpreter appeal to her. She has saved some money and her parents are willing to help her with tuition costs and living expenses.

In small groups, discuss Angela's options. Try to come to an agreement about what she should do or rate the different options. You can list advantages and disadvantages (pros and cons) for each option, if you wish. After the discussion, each group should report its decision to the class, summarizing its main arguments.

OPTIONS

Metro University
MU is a large university in Angela's home city. Since housing costs are high in the city, Angela would have to continue to live with her parents if she attends this university. The university has a good reputation as one of the most important universities in the country but she has heard students criticize it for being too large and too impersonal. A new program combining linguistics and computer studies is being offered; this course of study looks interesting but is too new to show results in terms of job prospects afterwards.

City College
This is a large college in Angela's home city. It has a good reputation for practical training. Studies in computer science lead to well-paying technical jobs. Again, to attend this school Angela would have to live at home with her family.

Confederation University
This university is in a smaller city in the province, about 200 km from Angela's home. It has a good reputation for humanities courses and has a well-known teacher's college affiliated to it. Angela has been offered a scholarship that would cover her tuition. She could live in residence in first year and get an apartment afterwards.

Management Training
Angela has been offered a permanent position with the large company for which she has been working in the summertime. She would be able to work her way up in the company and continue her studies part-time in night school. At first she would have a junior position but there is good potential for rising in the ranks to senior management.

Travel
Angela has been offered a job that would entail lots of travel and therefore would not allow her the option of taking more courses. The pay is not very good, but she could see the world and also improve her languages.

Marriage
Angela has been dating a friend of the family who is older and wishes to settle down and start a family. He has proposed marriage but would like a traditional stay-at-home wife. He does not think that Angela should pursue post-secondary education.

Additional Vocabulary

nursery school school for children under the age of five

elementary school Kindergarten and Grades 1 – 6 or 8

junior high school Grades 7 – 8 or 9

secondary school, high school Grades 9 – 12 or 13

seminars small discussion groups

workshop class where students have an opportunity to practise skills

degree rank or title given by a university to a student who fulfills particular requirements

Bachelor's degree (B.A., B.Ed., B.Sc., etc.) first university degree attained after three or four years of study

Master's degree (M.A., M.Sc., etc.) university degree acquired after Bachelor's degree

Ph.D. or doctorate third university degree, entitles the student to use the title "Dr." before his or her last name

undergraduate student working on his or her first degree (Bachelor's)

graduate student a student working on a Master's or Ph.D.

correspondence course home-study course; materials and assignments are mailed out

tutor private teacher or assistant teacher

play hookey miss school deliberately

Discussion Topics

1. Compare the Canadian educational system with that in your country.

2. What is your opinion of university and college admission requirements for foreign students?

3. Are you in favour of standardized testing? Should students write university entrance exams?

4. What are the advantages and disadvantages of being a teacher?

5. How are computers changing education today? Do you think that computers could replace teachers? Why or why not?

Additional Activities

1. In pairs, develop and role play a dialogue in which a student and a counsellor discuss problems related to course changes, marks or career decisions.

2. Hold a classroom debate on one of the following topics:
    a) A university education should be available to everyone at minimal or no tuition fees.
    b) A child's education should be determined by the parents and not by the government.
    c) Standards of education should be stricter.
    d) Foreign students should pay the same tuition students as Canadian students.

3. In small groups, decide what you would do to improve your school.

Assignments

1. Find out about the different educational institutions in your area and what they offer in post-secondary and general interest programs.

2. Look through college and university calendars to find out what kind of programs are offered.

12

Language

A Broadcast Interview

When you are learning a language, it is often helpful to know something about its history. Native speakers take their own language for granted and do not realize how some of its features appear to learners. Knowing facts about English will not make it easier to learn, but it will help explain why the language works the way it does.

linguistics scientific study of language

hodge-podge (colloquial) mixture

baffles confuses

broadcaster announcer on radio or TV

print journalist journalist working in newspapers or magazines

Interviewer: And now we have an interview with Professor J. T. Lingo, Professor of **Linguistics** at Chimo University, who is here to talk to us about the growing business of teaching English. Good morning, Professor Lingo.

Professor: Good morning.

Interviewer: Professor, I understand that teaching English is becoming "big business" all around the world.

Professor: Yes, indeed. It seems that language schools are springing up everywhere and that a lot of Canadians are going overseas to teach English.

Interviewer: Why is that?

Professor: With the move toward a global economy, English has become the most widely used language in the world. It is the language of business, aviation, science and international affairs and people find that they must learn English to compete in those fields.

Interviewer: And do people find English an easy language to learn?

Professor: Well, every language has something about it that other people find difficult to learn. English is such a **hodge-podge** of different languages — it's essentially Germanic but a lot of its vocabulary comes from French, and technical words stem from Latin and Greek. This feature makes English fairly adaptable — which is a good thing for a world language — but it causes irregularity in spelling and pronunciation.

Interviewer: English spelling **baffles** me, too. That's why I'm a **broadcaster** and not a **print journalist**. (laughs)

Professor: Yes, well, anyway, English also has the largest vocabulary. Often there are words for the same thing, one that is Anglo-Saxon and one from the French — like "buy" which is Anglo-Saxon and "purchase" which is from the French. The French word often has more prestige.

Interviewer: Anglo-Saxon?

continued

Norman Conquest victory of William the Conqueror, from France, over Britain

slang language not suitable for formal use; words and expressions often short-lived or particular to a certain group

colloquial everyday, informal language

dialects variations of the same language

Professor:	That's the word for Old English. The **Norman Conquest** in 1066 brought the French language to Britain and helped English evolve into the language it is today.
Interviewer:	I see. Is there anything else particularly difficult about English?
Professor:	Well, the idioms in informal English pose a problem for some students.
Interviewer:	Informal English?
Professor:	As with any language, there are different varieties: **slang, colloquial**, formal, written, as well as the different **dialects** — British, American and Canadian English.
Interviewer:	And how is Canadian English different from American and British?
Professor:	Well, Canadian English is closer to American in pronunciation and idiom. Some of our words and our spellings do reflect British usage, however. We wouldn't use the British term "lorry" for truck, but we have kept the "o-u-r" spellings in words such as "honour" and "colour."
Interviewer:	This has been very interesting, professor. I'm afraid we're out of time. It has been a pleasure talking to you.
Professor:	Thank you.
Interviewer:	We have been talking to Professor Lingo of Chimo University. And now back to Barbara.

Discussion

1. Do you agree with Professor Lingo's assessment of the importance of English and its relative difficulty?

2. Do you think there will eventually be one world language? Will it be English?

3. How does English influence other languages and other cultures?

Learning by Experience

Even among native speakers of the same language, misunderstandings are common. For example, the listener may think the speaker is referring to a different situation or may not understand the significance of what the speaker is describing. Communication depends upon more than knowing the meanings of the words.

Tony: Hello, Maria. My brother home yet?

Maria: No, but he should be here any minute. Have a seat. How was work today?

Tony: Pretty good. I think I'm starting to make friends. Some of the guys asked me if I wanted to go out with them tonight. They said they were going to do some painting, but I said I was too tired.

Maria: Painting? On a Friday night?

Tony: Yeah, painting something red, I think they said.

Maria: Oh — "painting the town red." It's an old idiom — it means going out for a good time.

Tony: Now it makes sense. I really have trouble understanding them sometimes. English is a crazy language — so many idioms. Why can't they just say what they mean?

Maria: Every language has idioms, Tony.

Tony: But English is so illogical. There aren't any rules. It doesn't make sense. Spanish is so easy and clear.

Maria: Sure — to native speakers of Spanish. Don't worry — English isn't that hard. You'll **catch on** to what people are saying.

Tony: **One of these years.**

Maria: I remember my first few days in Canada. One time I was standing at bus stop and a woman asked me how long I'd been there and I said, "Three weeks." She gave me a funny look and didn't say anything. I thought she was rude but now I realize she was just asking me how long I had been at the bus stop. I was so used to people asking me how long I had been in Canada, that I answered automatically.

Tony: But that's not all that embarrassing.

Maria: But that's not the only time I misunderstood someone. Those first few months were filled with mistakes and misunderstandings. Even though I'd studied English in Portugal, the people here just didn't talk the way I had been taught.

Tony: Maybe I should just throw out my grammar books and **start from scratch.**

Maria: I wouldn't go that far. I just think you have to listen to people talking as well as study from books.

---

catch on understand, see the significance of

one of these years (idiomatic) it will take a long time; it will seem like forever

start from scratch start with nothing

Discussion

1. What is the probable relationship between Tony and Maria?

2. What kind of experiences have they had learning English?

3. Describe a personal experience that became comical due to a communication problem.

4. When and how did you start learning English? What experiences have you had in your study? What do you find hardest to master in English?

LANGUAGE NOTES

NARRATIVE TECHNIQUES

Conversations often include narratives and short stories or anecdotes, relating something that happened to the speaker or something that the speaker heard about. These stories serve to give an example or to entertain the listener.

Just as different cultures have different writing styles, they also have different storytelling techniques. English is a concise language, and the style is often brief and to the point. Some cultures, on the other hand, favour embellishment and indirectness in a narrative style.

A story should suit the situation and make a point that will add to the conversation. A story can be introduced by such phrases as:

You'll never guess what happened...
That reminds me of the time...
You know, once,...
I remember when...

One important element in a story is a description of the setting. The listener needs enough information to understand the situation, but unnecessary details should be left out. The setting includes the place and time that the story took place.

In order to give enough information, but not too much, it is important to test the knowledge of the listener through such expressions as:

You know that new restaurant on Main Street? Well...
It was in Calgary — have you ever been there?
I heard a funny story yesterday. I was talking to Manesh Patel yesterday — do you know him?

The characters of the story should also be described or identified with as much detail as is necessary:

And then I said to Amanda — she's my boss — that...

Some pauses in a story are effective in creating suspense. The following phrases are common:

And you'll never guess what happened next...
And then — you won't believe this — he said...

To shorten details of a story, the following phrases can be used:

Well, to make a long story short...
I won't go into all that, but...

Listen to other phrases and techniques that speakers use to tell a story. Practise these techniques in class activities and discussion. Effective storytelling is an art, and can add a lot to a conversation.

REPORTED SPEECH

When telling a story, speakers often use forms of indirect or reported speech instead of quoting directly. When the verb in the main clause is in the past tense, it is necessary to change the tense of the original speech.

Compare the following examples of direct and indirect speech:

John asked, "*Are* you coming?"
John asked if we *were* coming.

Peter said, "I *want* to go to the library tomorrow."
Peter said that he *wanted* to go to the library tomorrow.

Susan asked, "*Have* you been here long?"
Susan asked if I *had* been here long.

Harry said, "We *will* be late."
Harry told her that they *would* be late.

If the verb in the main clause is not in the past tense, the tense of the original speech does not change.

She says, "I'll be going now."
She says that she'll be going now.

Similarly, for facts that are generally true, the tenses are not changed:

She said, "English is hard to learn."
She told me that English is hard to learn.

Change the following quotes into indirect speech and the indirect speech into direct quotes.

1. "Help, I need a hand!" Ken yelled.
2. Doug stated that he was tired of commuting between two cities.
3. "Come and get it!" cried the cook at the barbecue.
4. Barbara laughed and suggested that her brother should stop having so much fun and work a bit harder instead.
5. "Make sure your spelling is accurate in the essay," stated Simon.

Practise reported speech in the classroom in the discussions and activities. A quick exercise is to have one person in the class make a statement or ask a question, and then have another person report it.

CULTURE NOTE

In Canada, more than 15 million people have English as a mother tongue, more than 6 million have French, and almost 3 million have another language as their mother tongue. Officially, "mother tongue" is defined as the language first learned in childhood and still understood. This is an important definition, because it differentiates "mother tongue" from "first language," which is the language that someone is most comfortable speaking. For most second generation immigrants, therefore, the first language is English or French while the mother tongue is the native language of their parents.

Language is an important issue to Canadians. Since Canada has two official languages — French and English — Canadians are entitled to information and services from the federal government in either language. However, the status of the French language has declined due to the dominance of English in North America. Today with English becoming such an important global language, the position of French in Canada is even less secure. Laws in this country reflect this concern. In Quebec, the Commission de la langue française regulates the use of French in the province. It demands that official signs and documents be in French, that the use of anglicisms in the language be controlled, and that French language studies be encouraged.

Language issues in Canada, though, cover more than the two official languages, French and English. More than 50 Aboriginal languages, such as Cree and Inuktitut, are spoken in Canada; unfortunately, several are in danger of dying out. In the past, Aboriginal children were neither allowed to use their mother tongue in school nor encouraged to learn it. Today, however, with the heightened awareness of Aboriginal rights and heritage, the study of Aboriginal languages is promoted.

Immigrants to English-speaking Canada bring with them a variety of languages. They may attend classes to learn English as a second language, but their children will be educated in English and use it as a first language. How much of their native language the children retain depends on a number of factors. For example, first-born children often know the native language better than their siblings. If the parents understand English well, often bilingual conversations will take place where the parents speak the native language and the children answer in English. Many school boards offer heritage programmes so that second-generation immigrants can study their native language.

In general, Canadians recognize the value of speaking more than one language. Children may begin learning a second language as early as kindergarten or nursery school. Adult education centres offer courses in a variety of foreign languages and special language schools are flourishing across the country. Surveys show that even Canadians who object to the costs of maintaining official bilingualism want their children to learn French or English as a second language.

Language and culture are intertwined; one cannot exist without the other. Language determines ethnic identity more than behaviour, food, dress, religion, social customs or geography do. That is why linguistic issues are so important in the world, especially in a multicultural country such as Canada.

LESSON PLANNING

In small groups, plan an English lesson for a beginner or intermediate class of ESL students. Choose one of the situations below and then make a list of vocabulary and useful expressions to teach. Plan a classroom activity to suit the student group.

SITUATIONS

1. A kindergarten class in one of your native countries about to have its first English lesson.
2. A group of business executives from overseas who speak English at an intermediate level but wish to brush up their skills in order to prepare for a business lunch with Canadians.
3. A beginners' class of new immigrants learning a lesson in survival skills (choose a lesson in banking, shopping, asking directions or other such skills).
4. A group of students in an overseas country who are about to come to Canada to study.

CLASS LEXICON

Teach your classmates a few phrases from your native language or another language you know. Make a chart similar to the one below, with words and phrases from the languages spoken by the students in your class.

Hello.	Good-bye.	Thank you	I'm sorry, I don't speak English.
Bonjour.	Au'revoir.	Merci	Je regrette, je ne parle pas français.

Additional Vocabulary

francophone French-speaking person

anglophone English-speaking person

immersion classes classes in which students are completely surrounded by or "immersed" in another language and culture

jargon specialized, often technical, words used in a profession (e.g., legal jargon)

anglicize to make or become English in form, pronunciation or character

Discussion Topics

1. If you could learn another language, which language would you choose and why?

2. Compare two languages that you are familiar with in terms of relative difficulty, use of idioms, pronunciation or other features.

3. What anglicisms appear in your native language? Do you think that using English words in another language is harmful or helpful?

4. Discuss how other countries have dealt with language laws. For example, has one language been made the official language and the use of other languages discouraged?

5. Discuss the use of French and English in Canada. Do you know of other countries that have more than one official language? What are the advantages and disadvantages?

6. Does becoming bilingual change a person? In what way?

7. Do you think children of immigrants should be encouraged to keep their mother tongue?

Additional Activities

1. Hold a classroom debate on one of the following topics:
   a) An official agency should be set up to rule on what should be considered acceptable English.
   b) There should be only one official language in Canada.
   c) All educated, professional people in the world should learn English.
   d) The world would be a better place if there were one official language, such as English or the artificial language Esperanto.

2. Play some word games in class, such as Scrabble, crossword puzzles and wordsearch puzzles.

3. In small groups, make a list of unusual English idioms that you have learned.

Assignments

1. Read up on the history of the English language.

2. Find out more about the laws governing the use of French and English in Canada and in your province.

3. Find a native speaker of English who wishes to learn your native language and exchange tutoring or hold conversation sessions.

13

Travel and Tourism

Sightseeing

When visiting a new city, tourists often find it difficult to know where to go and what to see. Tourists want to make the best use of their time, since they are usually not in town long enough to see most of the sights. Although brochures and tourist information centres are helpful, people who live in the city or who have visited there often are usually the best source of information.

This dialogue takes place in Ottawa, at an outdoor cafe on Sparks Street Mall. Yuri and Kirsten are sitting at a table looking over maps and tourist brochures. Lynn and Bill are sitting nearby.

cooped up (slang) confined, locked up

hit-or-miss haphazard, careless

browsing looking around without a specific purpose, for enjoyment

Kirsten: I don't know, Yuri. There's just so much to see and so little time.

Yuri: Well, we do have to make up our minds. This afternoon we could go to see the National Gallery or the Museum of Civilization or...

Kirsten: It's too nice a day to be **cooped up** in a museum.

Yuri: Well, let's see what else we could do...

Bill: Excuse me, we couldn't help noticing that you're new in town. Do you need any help?

Yuri: It would be nice to get a personal opinion on some of this stuff. We've never been to Ottawa before and the brochures make everything sound so terrific.

Lynn: I know what you mean. Sightseeing can be such a **hit-or-miss** thing.

Kirsten: We'd like to do something outdoors but not just wander around aimlessly.

Bill: Have you seen the old market area yet? It's my favourite part of the city — a lot of renovated historical buildings and reconstructed courtyards with different shops, boutiques, market stalls...

Lynn: You know, they have free guided walking tours of the area — a nice way to get an introduction to a place. Then you can stay and do some **browsing** on your own afterwards.

Kirsten: That sounds like a great idea. It would be nice to have a guide to explain things, instead of always looking up the information in a brochure.

Yuri: So where do these tours start?

Bill: Right in front of the Parliament Buildings. Just go up Sparks two blocks, turn left on Metcalfe, and there should be signs on the corner of Metcalfe and Wellington.

Yuri: Great, thanks a lot.

Discussion

1. How do you think Bill and Lynn knew that Yuri and Kirsten were new to the city?

2. Do you think a walking tour is a good way to see a city? How do you like to get to know a new place?

3. Change the location of this dialogue so that it is in your city or region. Make the necessary changes and perform it for the class.

4. In pairs, practise giving directions to various places. Use different kinds of maps (province, city, campus, buildings) to help you.

5. Discuss your experiences meeting people when you were travelling. Did strangers give you directions or help you out in any way? Would you offer help to someone who looks lost in your city?

A Trip to the West Coast

Vacations offer an interesting topic of conversation for friends and acquaintances. Travellers often send postcards to their friends and bring them back a small gift or souvenir. Showing pictures, slides, or videos from a trip is also common.

you know what they say an expression used to introduce a saying or proverb; "they" refers to people in general

time flies time goes by quickly

breathtaking exciting or wonderful

touristy slang adjective form of "tourist"

ferry boat that transports cars and people

seasoned travellers experienced travellers

I better reduced spoken form of "I'd better"

totem pole poles carved by some northwest coast Aboriginal peoples

souvenirs small items to remind travellers of the places they have visited

Fatima: Oh hi, Julie. Finally back from your vacation, I see.

Julie: What do you mean, "finally"? I feel like I've only been gone for two days instead of two weeks.

Fatima: Well, **you know what they say** — "**Time flies** when you're having fun." You did have fun, didn't you?

Julie: Oh, it was marvelous. B.C. is so beautiful. And it was so nice to get away from this cold, miserable weather. And those mountain views — they were absolutely **breathtaking**.

Fatima: How was Vancouver?

Julie: Busy. So much to see and do there. It was nice to take an urban holiday for a change, although next year I'll be glad to go camping again.

Fatima: So what all did you do?

Julie: Oh, we went to Stanley Park and the aquarium, up Grouse Mountain and to museums and galleries. All the usual **touristy** things.

Fatima: Did you get over to the island? It's only two hours away by **ferry**, isn't it?

Julie: Yes, it was funny how on the ride over, everyone stayed out on deck to enjoy the view, but on the way back, we just sat inside like **seasoned travellers** and read magazines!

Fatima: Victoria is a city I've always wanted to visit. They say it's such an elegant city with a lot of British influence.

Julie: We liked Victoria so much that we stayed on a day longer than we had planned.

Fatima: Oh, well, one of these days I'll get there myself. In the meantime, **I better** get back to work.

Julie: Before you go — I got you this pin for your collection.

Fatima: A tiny **totem pole**! It's beautiful. Thank you very much.

Julie: You're welcome. Maybe you can come over on the weekend and I'll show you my pictures and my **souvenirs**.

Fatima: Sounds great.

Discussion

1. Where do you think this dialogue is taking place? What is the probable relationship between Fatima and Julie?

2. Has Fatima ever been to the west coast of Canada?

3. Change the dialogue so that Julie has just come back from a visit to a city near where you live. Practise variations of the dialogue in pairs.

4. Give a short oral presentation to the class on a place you have visited or a place you would like to visit.

5. What kind of holiday do you prefer — sightseeing in a city, camping out or relaxing in a resort?

LANGUAGE NOTES

SYLLABLE STRESS

While some languages have regular stress patterns, English syllable stress is virtually unpredictable. As English has adopted words from so many languages, it has also adopted and adapted the spelling, pronunciation and stress. Since the stress is not regular, it has to be learned with each word. Dictionaries usually have the primary stress marked in word entries.

A stressed syllable is pronounced louder, longer and higher than other syllables. A misplaced stress can make a word unrecognizable. However, stress can also vary in English. A word may be stressed on one syllable in England, but on another in North America. The pronunciation of a word can change over time. And individuals have their own pronunciation patterns.

Practise the following Canadian place names. The primary stress is marked for each word.

Cánada	Saskátchewan	Hálifax
Torónto	Montreál	Wínnipeg
Óttawa	Albérta	Ontário
Vancoúver	Néwfoundland	Manitóba
Édmonton	Chárlottetown	

TAG QUESTIONS

Tag questions are interrogatives attached to the end of a statement. They request agreement or confirmation:

> That was a good concert, *wasn't it?*
> The bus leaves at seven, *doesn't it?*

Tag questions are formed with the auxiliary verb (or the verb *to be*) and a pronoun subject.

The tags for "I am" and "let's" are not regular:

> I'm invited too, *aren't I?*
> Let's go, *shall we?*

It is important to use a contraction in a negative tag question. Uncontracted forms are extremely rare and sound very formal:

> That tour company has a good reputation, *does it not?*

A tag question is used to make polite conversation. It requires a yes or no answer and is often used where a direct question would be inappropriate:

> It's a nice day, isn't it?
> The band plays well, doesn't it?

When a tag is simply asking for agreement, the intonation is rising-falling as in standard statements.

Sometimes the speaker uses a tag to get confirmation of a fact he or she is not quite sure of:

> It's two hours by ferry, isn't it?

In this case, the rising question intonation is used.

The "eh?" that many Canadians use after sentences has the same uses as a tag question. The "eh?" is considered characteristic of Canadian English and it is said that the presence of the "eh?" in someone's speech can help to distinguish a Canadian from an American.

Add tag questions to the following sentences:

1. Pamela has travelled to Korea and Japan.
2. The Mozart Festival was simply marvelous.
3. The plane leaves before noon.
4. There are several different routes to Yellowknife.
5. Retirement is a great time to plan a trip around the world.
6. Joseph spends half the year in Victoria.
7. The bus will be late.

USE OF "BEEN TO"

In the perfect tenses, *been* can be used as a past participle meaning "gone." The two participles have different meanings, however. *Been* means "gone and returned," whereas *gone* does not carry the additional meaning of a return:

> Sheila has been to the art gallery. (She has returned.)
> Ken has gone to the jogging track. (He has not come back yet.)
> Have you ever been to Montreal?
> No, I haven't been there before.

Complete the following sentences with either *been (to)* or *gone (to)*.

1. It's been a long day. Warren's _____ home.
2. That kid has _____ the corner store four times today.
3. The chairman of the Community League has _____ several political conventions in town.
4. Henry has _____ back to working as a political organizer.
5. Have you ever _____ Ottawa?

CULTURE NOTE

Tourism is a major industry in Canada. Canada is a vast country with a large choice of scenery and sites within its boundaries. Since the country is so large, Canadians are used to travelling long distances, even for a weekend. But because it is difficult to see all that the country has to offer, Canadians sometimes find it easier and cheaper to travel outside the country, especially to the United States.

During the winter, thousands of Canadians flock to warmer climates for vacations. Florida, California, Hawaii, Mexico and the Caribbean are popular winter vacation spots. Since Canada is a country of immigrants, visits to their native countries also account for many Canadians' trips abroad.

Just as many Canadians travel by crossing the border into the United States, so Americans make up the majority of the visitors to Canada. Canadians are generally well-informed about the U.S. because of the influence of the American media. In fact, many Canadians know more about American history and culture than about their own country. In contrast, Americans often know very little about Canada. Modern Canadian folklore is full of stories about tourists expecting snow in July or wanting to go to Prince Edward Island for an afternoon from Ontario.

Canadians also have much to learn about their own country, their own backyard as well as the far corners. For example, they may live in a city for years without seeing the local museums. They may visit local sites only when they have out-of-town visitors to show around their area.

Since accommodation is an expensive part of travelling; many alternative ways of taking

vacations are aimed at saving this expense. For example, staying in a hostel, a university residence or a bed-and-breakfast costs less than staying in a hotel or motel. Camping just outside a city allows vacationers to combine urban and country attractions. Some people take holidays with a house exchange, swapping homes with another family in a different city or country. Time-sharing allows people to invest in a vacation spot in a resort which is theirs for a week or two every year. Stay-at-home vacations give people the opportunity to indulge in visiting attractions, restaurants and theatres in their local area.

Within Canada, vacationers are offered a wide range of holidays. Some are lured by the wilderness, and camping, canoeing, and hiking are popular outdoor activities. Canadians take pride in the varied landscape and climate: the barren north, the majestic mountains of the west, the coastal fishing villages of the East Coast, the huge expanse of the prairies.

The urban areas in Canada provide interesting contrasts to the "great outdoors" and reflect the common attractions of populated areas. Vacationers enjoy all the advantages of city life — the theatre, galleries, restaurants, libraries and clubs. Canadian cities enjoy a reputation for cleanliness and an abundance of greenery.

Each Canadian city has something different to offer, from the old-world sections of Quebec City and the national museums of Ottawa to the modern western flavour of Calgary and the stately charm of Victoria.

CANADA TRAVEL PUZZLES

Working in pairs or small groups, solve the puzzles that follow. Afterwards, you can make your own quiz or puzzle for your classmates to try. Use the ones here as a guide. You can use other places in Canada as your theme or use other travel and transportation topics.

LOCATION MATCH-UP

Match the descriptions of the tourists attractions to the city or province where they are located. More than one site can match one location. Be as precise as possible — in other words, don't match a site with the province if the specific city is listed. Don't worry if you are not familiar with all the places given — work together with your classmates, take educated guesses and look for clues in the names or descriptions of the tourist sites.

Anne of Green Gables house — house that served as the model for Anne Shirley's home in the famous Lucy Maud Montgomery book

CN Tower — world's tallest free-standing structure

Fortress of Louisburg — reconstruction of eighteenth-century fortified town established by the French as a base to defend their settlements in the New World

Lake Louise — famous mountain lake whose turquoise colour comes from the rock flour in the water carried down from glaciers

L'Anse aux Meadows — first site of Viking settlement (1000 A.D.) in North America

National Gallery — main Canadian art gallery

Olympic Stadium — site of 1976 Olympics

Pacific Rim National Park — park whose boundaries extend off-shore to protect marine environment

Peggy's Cove — famous picturesque fishing village

Plains of Abraham — site of 1759 battle between the French and English

S.S. Klondike — restored paddlewheel boat similar to those used in the Gold Rush

Stanley Park — large urban park that contains a zoo and an aquarium

Thousand Islands — a group of over 1000 islands, two-thirds of which are Canadian

Tyrrell Museum of Palaeontology — dinosaur museum located in the Badlands, where many dinosaur fossils were discovered

Upper Canada Village — replica of a community from the nineteenth century

Alberta

Montreal

Newfoundland

Nova Scotia

Ontario

Ottawa

Prince Edward Island

Quebec City

Toronto

Vancouver

Vancouver Island

Yukon

CROSSWORDS

Use the clues to fill in each of the words that goes across. The blocked off squares going down will give the location of the sites.

1. the largest city in Canada
2. the world's largest waterfall by volume
3. tall tower which has revolving restaurant and transmitters for radio and TV signals
4. baseball team in Canada named after a bird
5. a group of five large lakes
6. a show, a large summer fair with agricultural displays and a midway, the "E" in C.N.E.
7. the capital of Canada

WORD SEARCH

The words listed are in the puzzle diagonally, horizontally, or vertically. They can be backwards but all the letters must be in a straight row. Circle the words you find.

Afterwards, look at maps of the Prairie Provinces to locate the place names. Check your dictionary and encyclopedia to define any of the other words you are unfamiliar with.

The following words are hidden in the puzzle:

ASSINIBOINE	CALGARY	GLENBOW	MOUNTIES	SASKATOON
ATHABASCA	CHURCHILL	HOODOOS	OILERS	STAMPEDE
BANFF	CREE	JASPER	REGINA	WINNIPEG
BLACKFOOT	EDMONTON	MOOSEJAW	ROCKIES	YELLOWHEAD

The Prairie Provinces

```
N M Q J E R W O B N E L G M S O Q N R
F G E C A L G A R Y Q V E T L C C W V
H T B S Q X F M Y M E R A R M K I C O
W J O E X M T K R E O M E E Y N Q H F
X W U O N V R R O P U Z P N G M K Q
X R U A F X A C K E C P N I S W J O B
U D E J S K Y X D N Y K P T F A I I R
M T I G L S C E Y G N E I A I L J H W
R M B L I L I A L E G O C E E E U W K
X R G Z A N I N L E L S O R S U S V Q
A J Y O M O A H I B A L S T D J I G I
S O O D O O H U C B A N O N A U D E W
V D D I J F W E A R O Q O W J K E M M
W Z R G S F F H P V U I I T H U S D V
W U L Y I D T N O P N H N D N E X A V
L T G L U A Q D A I U V C E B O A F S
K L I N M P Z L L B W Z J C Q R M D Q
S Y M O O S E J A W M E I M W Y I D X
P B H G B P D S C L F V V J F M Z P E
```

Additional Vocabulary

People get   on a bus
              on a train
              on a plane
              on a ship

but   in a car
              in a taxi

People go   by bus
              by train
              by plane
              by ship
              by car
              by taxi
              on foot

board   get on a ship, train, plain, bus

disembark   leave a ship or aircraft

deplane   leave an aircraft

taxi   to go along the ground or water under an air-craft's own power before or after flying (before "lift-off" or after "touch-down")

check in, check out   official arrival and departure in a hotel

hitchhike   to travel by asking rides from motorists along the road, to "thumb a ride" (slang)

motel   roadside hotel or group of cottages for people travelling by car (often with a separate entrance for each room)

inn   hotel, often a small hotel (used in names, e.g., "The Convention Inn")

hostel   lodging for travellers, usually members of a hostelling organization (often does not have individual rooms and bathrooms)

resort   holiday or vacation area, usually at a beach or in the mountains

cruise   pleasure trip on a boat or ship

return trip   two-way trip (there and back), round trip

Discussion Topics

1. What are the benefits of travel? What are some of the difficulties?

2. If you could travel to any place in the world, where would you go for a holiday?

3. What tips would you give to a new traveller?

4. Describe some of your more humorous travelling experiences.

5. What tourist sites are you familiar with in your city or area?

Additional Activities

1. In pairs or small groups, develop and role play a dialogue in which you ask a travel agent for information about the following:
   a) a flight to Yellowknife;
   b) a reservation on a bus tour to Jasper, Alberta;
   c) hotel reservations in Vancouver, B.C.;
   d) an inexpensive flight out of Montreal to London;
   e) a berth on a transcontinental train.

2. Make a short presentation to the class describing a region in Canada. Use brochures and pictures from books in your presentation.

3. In small groups plan a new tourist attraction for your city or region. Possible attractions include a museum, theme park, opera/ballet house, theatre or music hall, mega mall, historic village, amusement park, zoo, provincial park, aquarium, downtown shopping area or boat cruise. Present your idea to the class.

4. Go on a class outing to a tourist site near your school. Be sure to ask questions and use the maps and guides. Discuss your trip afterwards. Was it a useful outing? Discuss how good the visitor facilities are at the site. Would you recommend it to tourists?

Assignments

1. Plan a short trip around your province, highlighting places of information. Obtain information from the tourist office or travel agent to help you make a detailed plan.

2. Visit a travel agent and obtain materials about various kinds of holidays (cruises, safaris, bicycle tours). Describe the holidays to the class.

3. Find out more about some of the Canadian tourist sites mentioned in this chapter. Obtain information from the library, tourist information centres and travel offices.

Running the Country

14

The State of the Country

Complaining about the government is a national pastime all around the world, although the degree of freedom to do so may vary. Criticisms may be in the form of news editorials or political cartoons, but the most common form is the everyday conversation.

bleeding us dry   taking all our money

pay hike   (informal) pay raise

perks   extra benefits in a job (e.g., a company car)

hot air   (slang) talk (especially promises) that does not mean anything

boot 'em out   kick them out, get rid of them

freeloaders — those who live on goods and money provided by others

minority government government where one party has less than 50 percent of the seats

cost of living index   raises that equal the rise of the cost of living

UIC   Unemployment Insurance Commission — people use the three letters colloquially when they actually mean unemployment insurance

anyways   (slang) anyway

gang up on   work together to defeat

non-confidence vote   the opposing parties vote against the ruling party

Marcus:	The blasted government's at it again. They're talking about raising the sales tax.
André:	But they're already **bleeding us dry**.
Marcus:	Yeah and then they'll just turn around and give themselves another **pay hike**. As if they don't get enough with all their benefits and **perks**.
André:	Those politicians! They promise you everything when they're campaigning and then when they get elected you find it's just a lot of **hot air**.
Marcus:	Wait until the next election — we'll **boot'em out**. That'll teach these **freeloaders**. That'll show 'em they can't get away with it.
André:	Good idea. But who's going to replace them? I can't tell one party from another, let alone one campaign speech from another. Once they're in power...
Marcus:	What we need is a **minority government**. Then the politicians will work harder. They'll give us better social programmes. Job incentives. **Cost of living index** on UIC. Higher minimum wage.
André:	Dream on, Marcus. **Anyways**, minority governments don't last long. A year or two. The opposition parties **gang up on** the government, force a **non-confidence vote** — wham! Then we'll be wasting more money on elections.
Marcus:	And listening to more hot air.
André:	You just can't win. Depressing, eh?

Discussion

1. Summarize the complaints that André and Marcus make about the government.
2. Do you agree with what André and Marcus are saying?
3. Discuss complaints that you have about the government.

The Candidate

Interest in municipal politics is often less than in federal and provincial afairs; the voter turnout for local elections is usually lower and people often do not know who their municipal representatives are. However, city and regional politics are concerned with a lot of down-to-earth issues.

Marta: Bill Yanovich has been saying that he doesn't want to run again next fall.

Diane: Yeah, I heard that his seat on city council will be coming **up for grabs.**

Thomas: So, who do you think the candidates are gonna be?

Marta: Well, I was thinking maybe Diane should run.

Diane: Me? Ya gotta be kidding!

Thomas: Hey, great idea! That council could use some **fresh blood.**

Diane: But I don't know anything about politics.

Marta: Sure you do. You made a great **PTA** president last year.

Thomas: Yeah, and anyone who can get that group to pull together**'s gotta be a natural.**

Marta: And you worked on Bill's campaign so you know something about the mechanics involved. And with the contacts you made, you could probably get a lot of his volunteers to work for you.

Diane: But what about my job?

Thomas: Leon can give you a leave of absence while you run.

Marta: Besides which — weren't you talking about changing jobs anyway? Something about needing more of a challenge?

Diane: (groans) My words are coming back to **haunt** me.

Thomas: And you've always been **civic-minded.** You've been involved in citizens' groups for all sorts of issues — the **dump,** the downtown development project...

Diane: But it's a big step from working on a citizens' committee to actually running for office.

Marta: I think you'd be a **shoo-in.** But why don't you talk it over with Bill and with your family and think about it.

Diane: Good idea. I'll at least consider it.

---

up for grabs available

fresh blood new people with new ideas

PTA Parent and Teacher Association, parents involved in school activities

's gotta be (spoken reduced form) has got to be, must be

natural a natural talent

haunt come repeatedly

civic-minded involved in community and political issues

dump garbage dump

shoo-in (colloquial) a sure thing, easy or certain to succeed

Discussion

1. Summarize Marta and Thomas's reasons why Diane should run for office.

2. What kind of advice would you give Diane?

3. Would you ever consider running for election? Why or why not?

News Broadcasts

With fewer people reading the newspaper, Canadians depend on radio and television broadcasts to find out what is happening in the world. These broadcasts can range from brief announcements to in-depth analysis of the news.

clear-cut logging logging that takes all the trees in an area

ecosystem system of plants and animals living together within an enviroment

old-growth forest forest of mature trees, perhaps several hundred years old

backlog uncompleted work

task force governmental group formed for a specific objective

quotas a certain number of individuals, a share of a group

affirmative action employment programmes to hire individuals from minority groups experiencing discrimination

"Another environmental group has joined the Native groups' blockade of logging roads in the disputed Long River region today. Cutdown Logging Company representatives say they are ready to take more forceful action against the demonstrators. Band leaders say that the federal government must settle their land claims before any logging takes place in that area. Environmental groups are supporting the band's claims because they feel that **clear-cut logging** in the area will mean damage to the area's **ecosystem** and the loss of an important **old-growth forest.**"

"American and Canadian trade officials are meeting in Ottawa this week to discuss changes to the free trade agreement. The Americans would like to remove the clause exempting cultural industries from the agreement. However, the Canadian government has sworn to protect film, magazines, book publishing and other cultural industries in order to maintain our country's cultural identity. An American official was quoted as saying that she does not see a difference between American and Canadian culture."

"The Ministry of Employment and Immigration has released a report suggesting changes to immigration policy. These changes would make it easier for landed immigrants and Canadian citizens to sponsor relatives as immigrants. They would also allow foreign students to apply for landed immigrant status once they have finished their studies. Proposals have also been put forth to deal with the **backlog** of hearings for those claiming refugee status, including the hiring of more judges."

"A recently released **task force** report on employment has recommended reforms targeted at women, minority groups, and the disabled. This report recognizes the problems inherent in legislated **quotas** for employment or promotion. Instead of demanding **affirmative action** programmes, however, it recommends that the Human Rights Commission be given new powers to encourage employment for disadvantaged groups."

Discussion

1. In your own words, summarize each news broadcast.
2. Discuss the issues presented in these broadcasts. What is your opinion about native land claims? About clear-cut logging? About the Canada-U.S. free trade agreement? About immigration policy? About affirmative action programs?
3. Perform a news show in your class. Use broadcast items that deal with various current events.

LANGUAGE NOTES

SWEARING

Swear words and their uses are often difficult to understand in a new language and culture. Translating or explaining swear words often poses problems; literal translations do not carry the same force as the original word. Different cultures use different kinds of words for profanity. Religious words are used in Canadian French, for example, while animal words are often used in East European languages.

Generally, particular swear words lose their forcefulness over time and are replaced by other words. Words like "damn," "Hell," and "God" are often judged as mild today, whereas they brought a much stronger reaction 50 years ago.

A swear word may also have several, often milder, variations. "Heck" is a form of "hell," and "darn" may be used for "damn." Other examples of mild replacements for swearing are: "fudge," "shoot" and "Holy Cow." These terms are often quite humorous.

Although some people commonly use swear words in their speech, swearing is not considered proper. It is better to avoid swear words rather than to use them and offend someone.

VOICED AND REDUCED "T"

A *t* between vowels or other voiced sounds is often voiced and reduced in informal speech. The resulting sound, called a "flap," sounds like a *d*, as in *butter, city, little, letter*. The *d* sound makes pronunciation easier, but it does not occur when a person is speaking slowly or emphatically. The *t* sound also remains when it begins a stressed syllable, as in *return*. Those learning English need not use the *d* pronunciation, but it is helpful to recognize it. This pronunciation is considered more common in North American varieties of English.

STRESS DIFFERENCES

Several pairs of words in English are distinguished in pronunciation by a difference in stress. *Dessert* and *desert*, for example, are two words that are often confused. There is a difference in stress, as well as in spelling and meaning.

A *désert* is an area of very hot, dry land.

A *dessért* is a sweet food served at the end of meal.

The following are examples of words that have a first-syllable stress if they are nouns, a second-syllable stress if they are verbs:

conflict
contest
contrast
decrease
increase
object
present
progress
subject

Practise the following sentences. Pay close attention to the marked accented syllables.

1. I'll condúct you to your room.
2. I'm concerned about your cónduct.
3. He's progréssing very well.
4. She's making excellent prógress.
5. The time for the flight conflícts with my last meeting.
6. There is a cónflict here.
7. The two coastal towns contrást sharply.
8. The cóntrast is very striking.
9. There are many cónverts to the health craze who are eager to convért others.

CULTURE NOTE

The question of national unity is the most important political issue that Canadians face. The make-up and organization of the country has been an issue since before Confederation in 1867, and separatist movements have always been part of Canada's history. This lack of unity is not surprising when Canada's geography and history are taken into account.

Canada's land formations and population distribution do not encourage national unity. Canada is the second largest country in the world but its population is only about 26 million. Moreover, most of the population is spread out in a narrow band within 200 km of the United States. Natural barriers such as the Canadian Shield and the Rocky Mountains make it difficult to establish road and rail links from sea to sea. Even with modern technological advances, communication between Canadians and travel across Canada are difficult.

As a result, Canadians are often more regionalistic than nationalistic; they may consider themselves to be citizens of a particular province or region, rather than of the country. Furthermore, the provinces have strong governments and Canadian politics is often a struggle between federal and provincial interests.

To add to the difficulties of geography and competing political interests, no sense of nationhood has evolved to take in all the different ethnic identities. While Quebeckers may form a distinct group with their own language and culture, the rest of Canada cannot be neatly labelled. "English-Canada" is a misnomer because, while the majority of the population speaks English, the culture is not predominantly English and includes both Aboriginal and various immigrant cultures.

Another problem that Canadians face in the search for a national identity is the overwhelming presence of the United States. American political and cultural influences dominate the globe; a country that shares the same language and a continent finds it even more difficult to resist. Canada has a historical basis for anti-American feelings: the majority of the first English settlers in Canada were United Empire Loyalists who came from the U.S. because they did not agree with the American Revolution. Since then, the desire to be separate from the U.S. has been a dominant feature of Canadian society and politics.

Despite these difficulties, most Canadians believe that

their country is unique, that it is worth preserving and that some way must be found to allow its citizens to work together. Politics, of course, is the arena where most of these struggles are visible.

In Canada, there are three levels of government: municipal, provincial and federal. At each level, voters elect their representatives, who hold office for a specific length of time. The Canadian parliamentary system is based on the British model. The House of Commons, for example, is made up of representatives who govern the country. The Senate, on the other hand, consists of members who are appointed by the Prime Minister. The three main political parties are the Liberals, the Progressive Conservatives and the New Democratic Party (NDP).

Some Canadians find the political arena extremely fascinating; others find it boring. Involvement in politics can vary from active campaigning to simply voting during an election. In Canada, it is every citizen's right to vote. The ruling party is judged on its past performance and, in an election, can either be voted out or receive a fresh mandate. Canadians recognize their responsibility in choosing competent government and, as a result, their discussion of political issues can make for controversial conversations.

FUNDING DECISIONS

Imagine you are cabinet members in the provincial government. At a caucus meeting, you are deciding which government projects will be stressed in the next throne speech and budget. A number of possible projects are outlined below.

Working in small groups, choose a project that you wish to support (making sure that each group has a different project). With your group members, make a list of reasons why this project is important.

When you are ready, start the caucus meeting and, with your group, argue for support for your project. After the presentations and discussion, each student should vote on which projects are the most important. Count up the votes and rank the projects from most to least important.

AIDS (or Cancer) Research Centre

Both health care and education are provincial responsibilities. A plan has been put forward to fund a research centre with a medical school in the university of the provincial capital. This centre would concentrate on finding a cure for AIDS (or cancer) and would monitor the efforts of scientists in other parts of the country and around the world. The provincial government would increase the grant to the university in order to run this research centre.

Day-Care Subsidies

With more government support of day-care centres, more lower-income families would be able to afford day care for their preschool children. With good

day-care centres available, parents could work to increase their income or to support themselves without welfare payments.

Drug Task Force for Provincial Police

With the increasing publicity that drug abuse has received in the media, governments have been pressured to deal with the problem. Although the major metropolitan police departments have special drug programs, these do not reach all the towns and villages and rural areas. Since the provincial police are responsible for these areas, it has been suggested that the provincial police have a special unit to deal with drug problems.

Expressway

A major roadway through the province's main metropolitan area would ease the traffic congestion that now exists. Although public transit has been increased, the roadway is still needed to handle commuting from areas not served by transit, commercial trucking and other vehicular traffic.

Home Ownership Savings Plan

With the cost of housing so high, people are finding it very difficult to save enough money for a downpayment on a home. This plan would allow people to get a tax break on money they set aside in a special home savings plan. This plan could only be used on a first home.

Housing for the Disabled

This plan allows tax deductions for building and refitting houses and apartments to allow disabled people to live more comfortably. For example, wheelchair ramps could be built and kitchen counters could be lowered. These adaptations would also allow more disabled people to live at home rather than in institutions.

Multicultural Centre

A plan has been put forward to establish a multicultural centre in the provincial capital. This centre would focus on many of the issues related to having a multicultural society, including human rights and racism. It would fund education projects and support multicultural festivals. It would help newcomers adapt to the community and its culture.

Provincial Museum

The existing provincial museum is small and in an old building that is sadly in need of repair. Many artifacts cannot be exhibited because of the lack of space. Moreover, the condition of the artifacts is poor because of the lack of proper temperature-controlled storage, and museum officials fear that the museum treasures will be destroyed. A plan has been put forth for a new provincial museum, which will serve as a major tourist attraction for the capital city and an important resource for students learning about the province's history.

Salary Increase for Members of Provincial Parliament

The provincial government members have not received a raise for several years. Their salary has not kept up with the cost of living. It has been argued that fewer people are willing to give up jobs in order to run for a seat in the provincial government, because of the poor pay. A 6 percent raise is suggested.

School for the Gifted

It has been proposed that a special school in the provincial capital could be established for students who show exceptional academic talent, especially in the areas of science and math. Although the educational system tries to provide equal access to educational possibilities for all, it is recognized that different students have different needs and talents. Existing programs that work within the schools themselves are considered inadequate. Business leaders insist that more able graduates are needed in order for Canada to compete in the global economy.

Subsidy for Recycling

The government would put financial support into recycling programs. New recycling plants would have start-up costs partially funded by the government and existing plants could get grants to make necessary improvements to their facilities and equipment. Municipalities would receive grants for their collection of recyclable goods. Research into new recycling processes would also be funded. The aim would be to reduce the amount of garbage going into landfill sites.

Additional Vocabulary

M.P. Member of Parliament

M.L.A. Member of the Legislative Assembly (provincial government)

M.P.P. Member of Provincial Parliament

Premier leader of the provincial government

constitution body of laws and principles according to which a country is governed

Charter of Rights and Freedoms code outlining the rights and duties of Canadian citizens

Discussion Topics

1. What do you think of the news reporting in Canada? Is it informative and objective, for example?

2. Why is politics considered a controversial topic of conversation?

3. What do you see as the future of Canada?

4. Compare political issues in Canada with those in your native country.

Additional Activities

1. Organize a mock election in class. Have different students run for office and make campaign speeches.

2. Hold a debate on one of the following political issues:
   a) The downtown core in our city must be revitalized.
   b) Capital punishment should be reintroduced.
   c) Taxes in Canada are too high.

Assignments

1. Using a phone book and other directories, make a list of useful government departments and organizations. Find out what they do and report to the class.

2. Identify a municipal, provincial or federal politician and research his or her political background.

3. Follow a current news story and compare coverage on television and in the newspapers.

15

The Marketplace

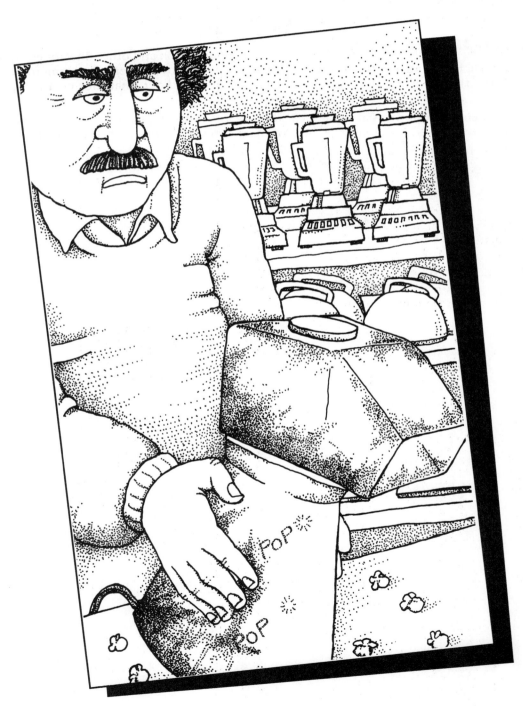

Customer Service

Making a formal complaint is one of the most difficult speaking or writing tasks, even for native speakers. Many people are reluctant to approach a manager or customer service representative when a service or a product is unsatisfactory. Knowing your rights as a customer and consumer and firmly asserting them is the key to getting satisfaction in your dealings with retailers and service providers.

The following dialogue takes place in a complaints department.

Employee:	Good morning. May I help you?
Customer:	Yes, I'd like a **refund** for this popcorn maker, please.
Employee:	I'm sorry — sale items are non-returnable.
Customer:	But this machine is **defective**. Look at it — it's all **scorched**.
Employee:	What happened? Did you read the instructions before using it?
Customer:	Of course I did. I read the booklet and followed the instructions exactly. But when I plugged it in, it started shooting popcorn kernels out all over the place. And then it started smoking so I unplugged it.
Employee:	It certainly does look burned out. Okay, I'll give you another unit and I'll send this one back to the manufacturer.
Customer:	I think I'd rather have my money back. It made quite a mess and I don't want to risk that again.
Employee:	Well, okay. I'll just check with the manager. In the meantime, could you please fill out this form?
Customer:	All right.

refund   money paid back, reimbursement

defective   faulty, having something wrong with it

scorched   having a surface burn, discoloured from burning

Discussion

1. What is the policy for returning items at this store?

2. Practise variations on this dialogue with a fellow student. Try to get a refund for different household items that are defective, or that are the wrong size or colour.

3. Have you ever had difficulty returning an item? Discuss your experiences with the class.

Redecorating

Large, expensive items such as furniture and appliances (so-called "big ticket items") are sometimes sold on monthly payment plans so the payments can be spread over a longer time.

However, many people prefer to pay for such purchases at once in order to avoid interest payments. Therefore, they budget and save for the purchase rather than yielding to impulse buying.

bonus   extra pay given as a reward

sprucing up   (colloquial) fixing up

for a rainy day   (idiomatic) for an emergency, for later need

easy chair — armchair; big, comfortable chair

Mary: Hey, honey, look — there's a big furniture sale on at Eaton's.

Hugh: Furniture sale? What do we need with more furniture?

Mary: Not more, new. We agreed to replace some of this old stuff if I got my **bonus**.

Hugh: You want to replace these beautiful antiques?

Mary: They're not antiques — they're junk. Look, this sofa sags in the middle, there are cat scratches on the drapes, and this armchair — well, even reupholstering won't help it.

Hugh: Okay, okay. You've convinced me. This place could do with some **sprucing up**. Let's see that ad. Hmmm, 50 percent off, eh? We can even pay in monthly payments.

Mary: But you always hate charging things. And we do have some money saved up **for a rainy day**, you know. I can at least start shopping around.

Hugh: We can both do the shopping — it won't be easy finding a replacement for my favourite old **easy chair**.

Discussion

1. How does Hugh feel about buying new furniture?

2. What financial considerations make this a good time for Hugh and Mary to buy?

3. In pairs, practise similar dialogues in which one student tries to convince the other that a purchase of a new item for the house is necessary.

Commercial Breaks

Television commercials can be annoying, informative, entertaining or humorous. They often contain inventive uses of language and provide cultural information. You can tell what is valued in the culture by what features are highlighted in the commercial. For instance, many companies stress how "environmentally safe" their products are.

"Tired of **static cling**? Do your clothes come out of the dryer all stuck together? Is it a shocking experience? Try new improved Softie fabric softener. Your clothes will come out soft and fluffy. No more annoying static cling. And the new April fresh scent will leave you thinking of the great outdoors. Buy new Softie today."

"**Mmmmm**, hot-out-of-the-oven muffins first thing in the morning — but no time to bake? No problem! New Bran Crunchie muffin mix is easy to make. Just add water and mix. Pour the batter in muffin tins, pop them into the oven, and **presto**! Fifteen minutes later you have hot delicious muffins. Even faster in a microwave. Start your day off right with the goodness of bran!"

"Are you losing your **edge** in the **boardroom** to younger-looking executives? Does your grey hair make you look much older than you are? Get back your image of youthful vitality by covering up that grey with Grey-Away. It's easy to use — just shampoo in. Your grey will disappear gradually. People will notice how young you look but no one will know why."

"For weeks all my kids talked about was getting one of those electronic game systems. But I didn't want them addicted to **mindless arcade games**. Then I heard about the CompuPal home computer — it's simple to set up and comes with a variety of software packages already installed. So now the kids are playing games — but they are learning math facts as they blast spaceships off the screen. They use the word-processing package for their homework assignments and a world atlas program makes geography fun. And the CompuPal is not just for kids. Balancing the home budget is easy with the electronic **spreadsheet** and **desktop publishing makes the club newsletter a breeze**. The CompuPal has opened up a whole new world for us — and it can for you too."

static cling clothes sticking together because of electrical charges

mmmmm (expression of delight) that's good

presto suddenly, at once (term associated with magicians)

edge advantage

boardroom where company directors hold meetings and make decisions

mindless not needing thinking

arcade games electronic games with a lot of action on the screen — chasing, shooting, manoeuvring figures and objects

spreadsheet table containing figures and calculations

desktop publishing designing and printing professional-looking documents (with graphics and different print styles) with the aid of a computer

make something a breeze make it easy

Discussion

1. Explain each commercial in your own words. What is being sold? What are the advantages claimed for the product?

2. What techniques are being used in the commercials to sell the products?

3. What qualities of the product are stressed in the commercial? What does this say about what is valued in Canadian society?

4. Describe a commercial that you find particularly effective. How is it effective? Is it humorous or annoying?

5. In small groups, develop your own television commercials. Perform them for the class.

LANGUAGE NOTES

STRESS FOR EMPHASIS OR CONTRAST

A stronger stress is given to words that need to be emphasized or contrasted in a sentence:

Put that *on* the dresser, not *in* it.
I'm going, too.
He asked for the *red* lamp, not the blue one.
I do *not* want to hear about it.
We're *biking* to the mall, not *driving*.

Practise the following sentences, emphasizing the italicized word.

1. No, I'll take the *blue* sweater.
2. Don't forget, the letters have to be mailed by *5:00* p.m.
3. She returned the *popcorn* maker, not the coffee maker.
4. Boys, I told you to go *around* the garden.
5. Then you *gently* insert the disk into this slot and pull the lever down.

USE OF "TO BURN"

The verb *to burn* can be used alone or it can be completed by different prepositions depending on the subject of the verb. The past participle can be *burned* or *burnt*, but *burnt* is more common in adjective forms:

The dinner burned while he was talking on the phone.

burn down — used for buildings destroyed to the foundations by fire:

That factory burned down years ago.

burn out — used for buildings or vehicles where the shell still remains:

That burnt-out building should be knocked down; it's dangerous.

burn out — used for electrical appliances, candles and matches that no longer work:

Is the lightbulb burned out?

burn-out — (idiomatic) used for people who are no longer able to work because of too much stress and over-work:

With the pressures of the school system, there is a high incidence of teacher burn-out today.

burn up — used for most objects that are completely destroyed by fire:

All the records were burned up in the fire.

burn up — (idiomatic) used for people who are angry

You mean he's late again? That really burns me up.

Place the correct expression in the following sentences.

1. It _____ me _____ when I wait half an hour for him.
2. The lamps on the street _____ last night.
3. I'm afraid Laurie just couldn't handle social work; she _____ after six months.
4. An arsonist likes to _____ buildings.
5. The trees were all _____ in the forest fire.

MONEY IDIOMS AND EXPRESSIONS

A wide variety of idioms and slang expressions have to do with the topic of money. For example, coins and bills have nicknames. When the dollar coin was introduced in 1988, the term "loonie" was introduced because of the loon pictured on the face of the coin. Other money nicknames are more established ("penny," "nickel," "dime," "quarter" and "buck") and are used in expressions. If something costs "a pretty penny," it is expensive, whereas items which are "a dime a dozen" are easy to get and of little value.

Slang words for money like "dough" and "bread" reveal the association between money and food. "To bring home the bacon" means to earn money for living.

There are a number of negative expressions for people who do not like to spend money; such people may be referred to as "miserly," "tight" or "cheap." Nouns that mean the same thing include "cheapskate," "Scrooge" and "penny-pincher." On the other hand, someone who spends too much money may be called a "spendthrift."

Other idioms related to money and shopping are illustrated in the following sentences:

He's not worried about the cost — he has *money to burn*. (so much money that he can burn it)
During the recession, we had a hard time *making both ends meet*. (earning enough to live on)
As treasurer, he has control of the club's *purse strings*. (finances)
The renovations will *cost us an arm and a leg*. (cost a lot of money)
I'm *flat broke* so I'm just going *window shopping*. (I have no money; to browse, to look at merchandise without buying anything)

CULTURE NOTE

Canadians, like Americans, are considered to be materialistic, yet they get mixed messages about their spending habits. For instance, the term "yuppie" (young urban professional) has a negative connotation because it focuses on the willingness of this group to spend a lot of money on high-tech gadgetry, designer clothing and other expensive consumer products. On the other hand, business and government tell consumers that spending money encourages economic growth. It is often pointed out that Canadians tend to save a lot of their income and that they are among the highest savers in the world.

Because most Canadians have easy access to the American marketplace, they often compare prices of goods in Canada to those in the United States. However, Canada is a more expensive country for business to operate in: the relatively low population spread over a great distance makes transportation and communication costs high.

Canadian consumers also complain about the federal and provincial taxes on items they buy. Some taxes are hidden (included in the item's sticker price) and others are sales taxes, charged when the item is purchased. Heavily taxed items include liquor, cigarettes and gasoline. Yet Canadians enjoy many government services and social benefits as a result of the income generated by taxes.

Since it is generally agreed that nothing comes cheap, shopping becomes a question of spending money wisely. Canadian consumers are constantly bombarded by various kinds of advertisements — in newspapers and magazines, on radio and television — and the choice of products can be overwhelming. Because of concern for the environment, Canadians have changed their buying habits. For example, disposable items are less popular today and consumers look for goods that will last a long time and will not have to be quickly replaced.

Canadians also try to save money by using coupons and by checking newspapers for advertisements of special sales. Second-hand stores, flea markets and garage sales have inexpensive used items. Shopping around for the best deal can be time-consuming but is often rewarding.

Although there are federal and provincial laws to protect the consumer from false advertising, high-pressure selling and below-standard products, it is still up to the careful consumer to avoid impulse buying and poor budgeting. Consumer groups test various products and publish lists of reliable products. Thus, the smart consumer is an educated one. An often-used Latin saying explains the situation well: caveat emptor — "let the buyer beware."

THE SELLING GAME

Divide the class into pairs. One person is the salesperson, the other the customer. The salesperson tries to convince the customer to buy something, while the customer resists. Some suggested sales items are given in the list below. You can also use items in the class as props and try to sell them. Students can switch roles, taking turns being customer and salesperson.

As much as possible, arguments should be answered with counter-arguments. For example:

Salesperson: This food processor will even mix bread dough.

Customer: But I prefer to make dough by hand. It's sticky and hard to clean from a machine.
Salesperson: Not if you soak the bowl and then put it in your dishwasher.

The dialogues can be performed in front of the class or in small groups. Students watching the dialogue may wish to discuss it, adding other arguments that could have been used. Dialogues can be judged for such features as "Most Aggressive Salesperson," "Funniest Salesperson," "Most Trustworthy Salesperson," "Most Stubborn Customer," "Fastest-thinking Customer," etc.

Items to Sell

air conditioner
bicycle
compact disc (CD) player
central vacuum or regular vacuum cleaner
computer
diamond ring
encyclopedia, dictionary or reference book
food processor
house or condominium
lawn care services
life insurance
microwave oven
music lessons
sports car
steam carpet cleaner
telephone answering machine

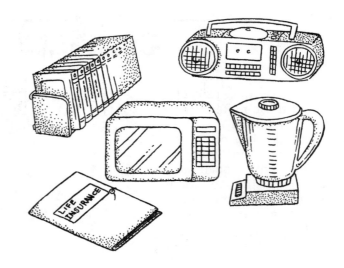

Additional Vocabulary

barter   exchange goods or services without using money

deposit   sum of money paid as a pledge or promise to buy

warranty   guarantee from a manufacturer or store to repair or replace defective items, often with a specific time period

scratch 'n dent sale   sale of items that are slightly damaged, usually with exterior imperfections that do not affect use

rain check   promise that a customer can buy an out-of-stock item at a later date and for the price originally advertised

rip-off   (slang) bad deal, where someone has been taken advantage of or cheated

in the red   operating at a loss (red ink is used to show a deficit)

in the black   operating at a profit

Discussion Topics

1. What kind of shopper are you? Do you like to shop? Are you a spendthrift or a penny-pincher (a spender or a saver)?

2. How do shopping practices here differ from those in your country, in terms of availability of merchandise, helpfulness of salespeople, financing, consumer protection, etc.?

3. What do you think is the best way to find a bargain?

4. What is your opinion of credit cards and other systems that replace cash?

5. Discuss the advantages and disadvantages of our commercially oriented culture. What are some problems that consumers and business people face?

6. Do you think prices in Canada are reasonable? Are the taxes charged fair?

Additional Activities

1. Find out what consumer complaints are currently in the news and debate one of the issues. Topics may include new taxes, shopping by-laws (such as Sunday shopping), the take-over or closing of major retailers, and the construction of large shopping malls.

2. Examine newspaper and magazine ads and radio and TV commercials. Analyze what makes them effective.

Assignments

1. Find out about the various consumer protection laws in your province or in the country.

2. Visit a shopping mall near you and make a report on the type of stores found there and how their merchandise is arranged.

16

On the Phone

Phone Calls

Many people dislike using the telephone, even though it is an essential part of modern life. Talking on the phone can be especially difficult for non-native speakers of English who rely on visual cues. Telephone conversations, however, include several ritualized expressions. Learning these expressions can make using the telephone less stressful.

1. For personal calls, it is often a good idea to check if the person you have called is busy or not.

   A: Hello.

   B: Hi, Joan. It's Margaret. Are you busy right now or do you have time to talk?

   A: Well, actually — I'm just on my way out the door to pick up Martin. Can I call you back this afternoon?

   B: Sure. I'll be in until 5.

   A: Okay. Talk to you later.

   B: B'bye.

2. Wrong numbers can be the result of dialling incorrectly or of writing down a wrong number. If you are not sure what the problem is, check the number with the person you have reached, but do not ask "What number is this?"

   A: Hello.

   B: Hello. Is Roger there?

   A: No, I'm sorry. You must have the wrong number.

   B: Is this 555-7039?

   A: No, it isn't.

   B: Oh, I'm very sorry for bothering you. Good-bye.

   A: Bye.

3. It is a good idea to offer to take a message if the person the caller asks for is not available.

   A: Hello.

   B: Hello. Is Jonathan there, please?

   A: No, I'm sorry — he's not in right now. May I take a message?

   B: Yes, could you please tell him that Philip Masters called? He's got my number.

   A: Okay, I'll give him the message.

   B: Thank you. Good-bye.

   A: Bye.

4. Self-identification is often done with the word "Speaking," which is a shortened form of "This is he (or she) speaking."

   A: Hello.

   B: Hello. Is Mr. Franklin in, please?

   A: Speaking.

   B: Good morning. I'm calling from Overleaf Bookstore. The book you ordered is in — *Amazing!* by Susan Bates.

   A: Fine — I'll come by and pick it up. Are you open Thursday evenings?

   B: Yes, until 9.

   A: Good. Thank you very much. Good-bye.

   B: Bye.

5. **"Telephone solicitation" is the term used to describe phone calls from businesses trying to get customers.**

   A: Hello.

   B: Good evening. This is Linda from Acme Carpet Sweepers. Your household has been specially selected for our special offer. You will receive a free gift and there is no obligation to purchase. One of our representatives will come by with your gift and will give you a demonstration of our new carpet care products...

   A: No, thank you. I'm really not interested.

   B: Are you sure? This gift will be yours to keep with no obligation.

   A: No, thank you. (firmly)

   B: All right then. Good-bye.

   A: Good-bye.

6. **People often put up notices in grocery stores or classified ads in the newspaper to sell items they no longer want. This call follows up on such an advertisement.**

   A: Hello.

   B: Hello, I'm calling about the freezer you have for sale. Is it still available?

   A: Yes, it is.

   B: Could you tell me more about it?

   A: Well, it's a small apartment-size chest freezer, in excellent condition, only two years old, and we're asking $100 for it.

   B: Oh, well, actually I had something larger in mind. Thanks anyway. Good-bye.

   A: Bye.

7. **Receptionists making appointments often need to know the nature of the visit in order to schedule time appropriately. They ask whether you are a new patient or client in order to know whether to pull your file out or make a new one for you.**

   A: Garneau Health Clinic. Please hold the line.... Hello, sorry to keep you waiting. May I help you?

   B: Yes, I'd like to make an appointment to see Dr. Hillis.

   A: Is it for something urgent or just a regular visit?

   B: Just a check-up.

   A: Would Thursday the 27th, at 2:15 be convenient?

   B: Yes, that's fine.

   A: May I have your name and phone number, please?

   B: Andrew Pearce, P-E-A-R-C-E. 555-8632.

   A: Have you seen Dr. Hillis before?

   B: Yes, I have.

   A: All right, we'll see you on the 27th then.

   B: Thank you. Good-bye.

   A: Bye.

8. **Usually fancier, more expensive restaurants require reservations while more casual ones do not.**

   A: Walden's Restaurant.

   B: Hello. I'd like to make reservations for dinner tonight. A party of four, at seven o'clock.

   A: Yes, that would be fine. And your name, please?

   B: Krentz. K-R-E-N-T-Z.

   A: Fine, thank you, Ms. Krentz. We'll see you then. Good-bye.

   B: Good-bye.

9. **With government offices it is a good idea to summarize the information you need in a short sentence so that you can be connected with the proper department or person.**

   A: Department of Forestry.

   B: Yes, I'd like some information about permits for cutting Christmas trees.

   A: Just one moment. I'll connect you with the right office.

   B: Thank you...

10. **Directory assistance often uses a recorded voice to give the phone number.**

    A: Bell Canada. What city, please?

    B: North Bay. I'd like the number for Murphy, M-U-R-P-H-Y, initial C.

    A: Do you have an address for that name, sir?

    B: I think it's on Forest Avenue — I don't have the exact address.

    A: (recorded voice) The number is 555-6047. I repeat, 555-6047.

11. **For collect calls, a zero is usually dialled before the number and the operator comes on the line.**

    A: Operator.

    B: Yes, I'd like to reverse the charges please.

    A: May I have your name please?

    B: Robert Peterson.

    A: Thank you. (ring, ring)

    C: Hello.

    A: I have a collect call from Robert Peterson. Will you accept the charges?

    C: Certainly. Hello, Bob...

12. Good news is often carried in personal phone calls.

A: Hello.

B: Hello, Amelia. It's Zula.

A: Hi Zula. How are you?

B: Just great today, thanks. I'm a grandmother!

A: Anya had her baby! That's fantastic!

B: A beautiful, healthy, 3.5 kilogram baby girl. Born just last night. They haven't decided on a name yet.

A: How's Anya doing?

B: Fine. Tired, of course. But the delivery was fairly straightforward. She was in labour for eight hours.

A: And how's your son-in-law taking it all?

B: Oh, he's on Cloud Nine. He coached Anya through the delivery and was thrilled that he got to see the birth.

A: I'm so happy for you all. I'll have to go see Anya and the baby, but I think I'll wait until she's home and settled in.

B: That's probably a good idea. I don't think she'll be in the hospital more than a day or two anyway.

A: Give Anya my regards and tell her congratulations from me.

B: Okay. Listen, I've got a lot of calls to make, so how about if I get back to you later.

A: Sure. Maybe we can get together for a coffee.

B: Great. Good-bye.

A: Bye.

13. Answering machines are a commonly used convenience.

A: Hello. You have reached 555-0909. We're sorry we can't take your call right now. Please leave your message after the beep.

B: Hi, André, it's Michael calling. I just wanted you to know that I booked the racquetball court for Tuesday at 7 p.m. If that time isn't convenient for you, call me back. Otherwise, I'll see you at the club on Tuesday.

14. Some areas have a common emergency number, 911, for police, fire and other emergency services.

A: Emergency.

B: I need an ambulance at 408 Jackson Drive — Jackson Meat Market. One of my customers seems to be having a heart attack.

A: I'm sending one right now, sir. 408 Jackson. Is there someone there who knows CPR?

B: Yes, my wife took a course. She's trying to help him now.

A: The ambulance will be there in a few minutes, sir.

B: Thank you.

LANGUAGE NOTES

LETTERS AND NUMBERS

It is important to give information clearly on the telephone. Names often have to be spelled. Even common names in English have different spelling variations. In spelling, it is important to pronounce the letters carefully. If there is a danger of misunderstanding the letter, a phrase such as "M, as in Mother" can be used for clarification.

The names of the alphabet letters are similar in many languages and can be easily confused. Vowels, for example, can be difficult to distinguish, particularly *E* and *I*. *J* and *G* can also be confused. In Canadian English, the last letter of the alphabet is usually pronounced "zed"; in American English, it is "zee."

Numbers also pose a problem. Check any numbers given by repeating them. Pairs such as "thirty" and "thirteen" are difficult for some people to distinguish. The "teen" numbers are pronounced with the stress on the second syllable. For example, compare:

thírty   thirteén

Note also that when a measurement is used as an adjective, the form becomes singular:

The boy is four years old.
He is a four-year-old boy.
The pole is two metres long.
It is a two-metre pole.

Practise the pronunciation of letters, numbers and dates in class.

TELEPHONE EXPRESSIONS

There are many common expressions used on the phone. For example, "Speaking" is the term used to acknowledge that you are the person asked for. "This is he" or "This is she" is sometimes used, but these phrases are quite formal.

Other commonly-used expressions include:

He's on another line right now. Would you like to hold?
She's not in right now. Can I get her to call you back?
You can reach him at 555-8242, extension 24.
I'd like some information on _____.
Could you give me some information on _____?
Would you mind repeating that?
Could you repeat that, please?

To end a social call, common expressions are:

Well, I'd better let you go now.
It's been really nice talking to you.
I'm afraid I'm going to have to run.

CULTURE NOTE

The following directions reflect telephone etiquette as understood by Canadians.

Residence phones are answered with a simple "Hello"; business phones are answered with the name of the business. If you do not recognize the voice of the person who answers the phone, do not ask "Who is this?" It is polite simply to ask for the person you are calling or to state the reason for the call. If you reach a wrong number, apologize politely.

Many businesses and charities try to get customers and sponsors through phone calls. These may even be computerized recorded calls. Some people object to this practice, because it is more intrusive than junk mail, especially since calls often come at dinnertime. Moreover, with these calls it is often difficult to verify the source of the call. When you get a call from someone you don't know, be careful about giving personal information, even your name. Some dishonest people use

the phone to find out when a home will be unoccupied or to get credit card numbers.

It is important to get to the point quickly when you are making a telephone call. When calling for information, do not give a complete case history to the first person that answers the phone. State the nature of the call and be sure you are connected to the right person before going into details.

Be sure to repeat phone numbers and other information

given over the phone. Do not be afraid to say, "I'm sorry. I didn't quite get that. Could you repeat the name, please?" If you don't understand a name given, ask for the spelling.

If a person is explaining something or giving information that requires a longer conversational turn, say occasional words of acknowledgement on the phone during the speaker's pauses. "Uh-huh" is used for a positive reaction; "uh-uh" is a negative one. If you are silent for too long, the speaker will wonder if you are still listening.

If an automatic answering machine takes your call, make sure you speak clearly and carefully in order that the message can be understood when the tape is played back. There are also answering services where a person will answer and take a message. Answering machines also allow people to screen their calls (to find out who is calling before they answer the phone).

Advances in communication technology mean that a wide variety of phone features and services are available today. For example, you can have calls forwarded to another number or have the number of the person calling displayed before you answer. Moreover, phone lines are used to transmit fax messages and modem communications between computers.

Canadians rely on the telephone, yet they often complain about it. The ringing phone often seems to be a rude interruption. Moreover, some people simply dislike talking on a phone. In personal communications, people rely on visual cues for part of the message. For instance, facial expression reveal people's feelings. Phone conversations are harder to understand because these visual cues are missing. Furthermore, the anonymity of the phone can be both an advantage and a disadvantage. It can give people the courage to say things they would have trouble saying face to face, but it can also encourage rudeness. Although video phones have been talked about for many years, many people feel that they would be an invasion of privacy.

A word about emergency calls: Keep emergency phone numbers handy, but do not misuse them. True emergencies require immediate assistance. Do not call emergency phone numbers for information. Police and fire stations often have two numbers: one for emergencies and one for regular business. Many regions and cities have a 911 emergency number system. If you require assistance (fire engine, police, ambulance), give your address right away. In the event you get cut off, they will at least know where to find you.

WHAT WAS SAID?

People often overhear someone having a telephone conversation and wonder what is being said by the other person. Imagine that you have overheard the conversation that follows. Working in small groups, try to reconstruct the conversation and fill in what could have been said by the other party.

Perform your completed dialogue for the class and compare it to the other groups' dialogues. (Afterwards — just for fun — perform a mixed-up dialogue; read the dialogue with each response given from a different group's dialogue.)

Hello.
_____

Oh, hi. What's new?
_____

So that's where you've been hiding. How was the trip?
_____

Uh huh.
_____

No, I've never been there.
_____

Sounds great. Maybe I should consider that for my next vacation.
_____

Okay. I'd love to see them.
_____

You're kidding! And then what happened?
_____

Uh huh.
_____

I don't believe it.
_____

Well, we'll have to see about that.
_____

By the way, have you heard from Garth recently?
_____

You're kidding. I thought he was a confirmed bachelor.
_____

That soon?
_____

Well, she seems nice enough but they really haven't known each other too long.
_____

Yeah, I know a long engagement is no guarantee of success. After all, look at my cousin and his wife.
_____

A party — that sounds like a great idea. Like an informal engagement party?
_____

We could have it here.
_____

Oh, it's not really any trouble. I have more room. We could get together this weekend and talk about it.
_____

Sure. That sounds great. See you then.
_____

Additional Vocabulary

Phrases describing the mechanics of a phone call:

> to look up a number in the phone book (or directory)
> to be on the line, on the phone
> to hang up at the end of a call
> to get a busy signal, the line is busy
> to dial the number (even with push-button phones)
> to be on hold
> to make a collect call, to reverse the charges
> to leave the phone off the hook
> a pay phone, a telephone booth

Discussion Topics

1. What do you notice about the way Canadians use the phone? Is it different in your culture?

2. What do you think of telephone solicitation?

3. Describe amusing experiences or problems that you have had on the phone.

4. Would you like to have a videophone? What are the advantages and disadvantages?

Additional Activities

1. Bring telephone books to class. Practise looking up various listings, in the white, blue and yellow pages. Look up doctors, restaurants, taxis and government offices, for example.

2. In small groups, work on telephone dialogues. Practise the calls that you are most likely to make. Include emergency calls and calls for information.

Assignments

1. Make an information call at home. Use the yellow pages to find a business listing and then make the call and report to the class on your experience.

2. Keep a record of the kinds of telephone calls you receive in a week.

3. Find out about the various telephone services that are available both for private homes and for businesses.

Index of Language Notes

Index of Vocabulary Notes